The Poverty of Multiculturalism

The Poverty of Multiculturalism

Patrick West

Introduction by

Kenneth Minogue

Civitas: Institute for the Study of Civil Society
London
Registered Charity No. 1085494

First Published September 2005

© The Institute for the Study of Civil Society 2005
77 Great Peter Street
London SW1P 2EZ
Civitas is a registered charity (no. 1085494)
and a company limited by guarantee, registered in
England and Wales (no. 04023541)

Email: books@civitas.org.uk

ISBN 1-903 386 46 2

Independence: The Institute for the Study of Civil Society
(CIVITAS) is a registered educational charity (No. 1085494)
and a company limited by guarantee (No. 04023541). CIVITAS
is financed from a variety of private sources to avoid over-
reliance on any single or small group of donors.

All publications are independently refereed. All the Institute's
publications seek to further its objective of promoting the
advancement of learning. The views expressed are those of the
authors, not of the Institute.

Typeset by Civitas
in Palatino 11pt

Printed in Great Britain by
The Cromwell Press
Trowbridge, Wiltshire

Contents

Authors

Patrick West was born in London in 1974 and graduated from Manchester University in 1997 with an MA in Cultural History. He has written for *The Times, Daily Telegraph, New Statesman, Spectator, Times Literary Supplement, Catholic Herald* and *Living Marxism* (LM). He is the author of *Conspicuous Compassion*, Civitas, 2004.

Kenneth Minogue is Emeritus Professor of Political Science in London University. He is a director of the Centre for Policy Studies (for which he has written *The Egalitarian Conceit* and *The Constitutional Mania*) and a trustee of Civitas for which he has written *Civil Society and David Blunkett*. He is an Honorary Fellow of the London School of Economics. He has written *The Liberal Mind* (1963, new edition published by the Liberty Fund 2001), *Nationalism* (1967), *The Concept of a University* (1974), *Alien Powers: The Pure Theory of Ideology* (1985), *Politics: A Very Short Introduction* (1995), *The Silencing of Society: The True Cost of the Lust for News* (1997) and *Waitangi: Morality and Reality* (1998). He has edited several books, including most recently *Essays in Conservative Realism* (1996), and contributed essays to others. In his academic persona, he has lectured and visited universities and research institutes in many countries, but he has also written columns for *The Times* and the *Times Higher Education Supplement*, as well as reviewing for the *Times Literary Supplement*.

Acknowledgement

Thanks are due to Damian Thompson and to Ed West for helping this book to happen, and to those who participated in the refereeing process, and whose comments were so helpful.

Introduction
Multiculturalism: A Dictatorship of Virtue

Kenneth Minogue

In the last half century, millions of Asians and Africans have migrated to Europe. This has posed considerable problems of social adjustment both for the newcomers and for the existing population. These problems are relatively minor, however, compared to something else that grew out of these migrations. I refer to the fact that the doctrine of multiculturalism has imposed nothing less than a dictatorship of virtue upon a previously free people. And this is a doctrine emanating not from migrants but from the heart of our civilisation itself. I propose to say something about both the virtue, and the dictatorship.

The virtue at first sight might seem to be 'tolerance', something of which the British people have had a supply no less abundant than that of any other population, and more than most. But tolerance was an old liberal virtue. In our modern world, what we might call 'holding your nose tolerance' has been found inadequate—indeed, positively insulting. The notional beneficiaries of tolerance demanded something better: namely, social acceptance. And a little further down the line has come the demand for something more: social inclusion. As the doctrine of tolerance began in the 1960s to turn into a morality of acceptance and inclusion, it also began to make claims about reality, and turned into multiculturalism, the belief that all cultures are equal in value.

The doctrine is that we must, on pain of committing discriminatory racism, regard every individual, and every culture in which individuals participate, as being equally valuable. Indeed, as the doctrine develops, we must not only share this opinion. We must regard people of all cultures with equal affection, employ them, make friends with them, promote them and include them in everything we do, in proportion to their numbers in the population. The doctrine ramifies in many ways—for example it finds intolerable the old familiar collective specialisations that come and go in human groups—Gurkhas in soldiering, black pre-eminence in sport, Irishmen in the Boston police, not to mention women in the caring professions. In a multicultural society, any such responsiveness to the facts of talent and temperament must give way to a precise representativeness in every sphere of life.

You might judge that this is merely a ramshackle codification of the respect for others that is familiar to us as good manners, and familiar also as the equality of opportunity so long valued in liberal politics. You would be wrong. Multiculturalism is a doctrine about purity of the heart. Sympathy for one culture rather than another, indicates an impurity of the heart. But the disposition human beings have to prefer some things to others is so powerful that this criterion would erect as the test of virtue something that is a human impossibility. And that is just the point. For if we constantly feel a set of emotions running contrary to those we have been persuaded (on pain of racism) we ought to feel, then we become entangled in a sense of guilt. We are revealed as unworthy. And the psychological power of the doctrine is enhanced by the almost sinister indifference people have to actually defining 'racism'. Any accusation of it seems to stick. Yet, is it a sentiment, an idea, a theory, a social policy, an action? And whichever of these things it might be, how do they connect together? Is there any difference between a reflex of antipathy to a culture, and a practice of assaulting those who belong to it? A similar indeterminacy will be found in our expanding 'phobia' family, as in 'Islamophobe.'

Multiculturalism, then, belongs to a family of antinomian beliefs with a long religious history behind them. The best-known examples are Puritanism and Communism. In both cases, a doctrine of the purity of the heart was advanced as transcending mere rules of right and wrong. And the result has always been to constitute an élite of the pure in heart who would, of course, need the power to reform society so that it fully shared this ideal purity. In this process of reform, Puritans became adept at sniffing out sin, or Satanism, and set about purging society of witchcraft. Bolshevik comrades experienced the fullness of proletarian solidarity, only to find that many comrades had to be purged because they could not help revealing signs of bourgeois weakness. It is the same with us in Britain. Everybody says we must celebrate the wonderful diversity of the new multicultural society coming into being, but all too many people exhibit symptoms of racism and discrimination. Racism is, of course, a motive, a movement of the heart, but the evil of racism is such that it may work even among people who are, at least consciously, pure of heart. In antinomian doctrines, there are many ways of being a sinner. This is why we have 'institutional racism'.

So much, for the moment, about the virtue. But why am I suggesting that Britain is experiencing a 'dictatorship' of virtue? The 'dictatorship' develops out of the way in which modern governments have developed. Anybody who cares for freedom will recognise modern British government as resembling a kind of giant octopus perched above society. On the one hand, it sucks up over half of all the wealth produced by the economy, and on the other hand redistributes this wealth through tentacles that reach down into the farthest corners of society—to schools, hospitals, charities, industrial enterprises, sports clubs, museums and films, media organisations and indeed right down to the domestic hearth and the introspections of its subjects through its concern with skills, bad practices such as smoking and eating the wrong food, and good practices such as counselling. There's always a demand for more money, and the Government has quite a lot to dispense. West End theatres, for example, are currently wondering whether to make a devil's bargain by accepting subsidies to improve their infrastructure.

Our governmental octopus is, of course, a benevolent creature, full of good intentions. Its tentacles grow ever longer because it dispenses subsidies to help social activities that have electoral appeal. Then a process develops: because taxation increases, individuals have less money for sustaining their own independent activities, and are tempted to seek funding from those ever-generous tentacles, leading of course to increases in taxation, which further reduce the independent resources in civil society, which ... and so on. First come the subsidies, and then of course come the demands for the accountable use of the taxpayer's money. Before long, social institutions have become hopelessly addicted to subsidy and can hardly imagine what a free and independent life would be like. The universities after 1920 had half a century of autonomy under the University Grants Committee before they fell under the juggernaut of the DfES. They always get you in the end. Other beneficiaries find themselves being rationalised much more quickly.

People sometimes talk of the inevitability of death and taxes, but these are as nothing compared with the rapidity with which those tentacles start pushing the beneficiaries of subsidy around. The expression 'civil society' referred in the nineteenth century to the whole network of independent social activities that were possible because the state was largely content merely to provide a framework of law and order. In the last century and more, however, the state has reduced most institutions—schools, universities, hospitals—to a condition of helpless dependence. The liberal democratic state has turned into this interesting octopus, sitting astride everything we do, and frightfully eager to help us with any project we might want to engage in.

The marriage between multiculturalism and big government was obviously made in heaven. Big government found in the multiculturalist passion for purity of heart a licence to extend its tentacles into areas it had not previously been able to reach, while multiculturalism found in the state the instrument of national purification it needed. The alliance had some of the features of the mediaeval relation between a guiding church and the secular arm enforcing its policies.

The problem to which this alliance responded was the coming of mass migration into Europe, largely from Africa and Asia. European societies had long been familiar with large-scale migration because Europeans had swarmed over Australia and the Americas from the beginning of modern times. The United States was a society almost entirely constructed out of migrants. The problem with post-1945 migration was that it involved people of different colours and religions. Cultural variation had sometimes led to tensions in the United States, but most of those migrants had come from more or less Christian Europe. In this new situation, the problems of having black and white, Christian, Muslim, Hindu etc., not to mention, in feminist times, men and women settling down alongside each other in modern liberal states were of a whole new complexity.

Libertarian economists often thought there was no problem at all; rising manpower facilitates growth. Nationalists often thought that migration was destroying the very conditions of toleration that made Europe such an attractive place. But the doctrine that soon established itself as dominant, both as a respectable sentiment and as the orthodoxy of state policy, was multiculturalism.

The multiculturalists explained to us that all cultures were equal. This vague expression might mean, what an anthropologist would certainly think, that every culture must be understood as a human response to a context and therefore as having moral value and intellectual interest in its own terms. But it might also mean that the cultures of the migrants to Britain were equal in all respects to that of the Europeans among whom they were settling.

Nobody in his senses believed that. Virtually everybody in Britain believes, and rightly, that whatever the shallowness and injustices of European life, it is superior to that of most other cultures. This powerful conviction results not merely from the fact that it happens to be the way of life with which we are familiar. It also arises because we regard our apparatus of rights and the rule of law as better than the Islamic Sharia, for example. Nor do we regard our disapproval of the ritual genital mutilation of young girls, something prevalent in parts of East Africa, as a mere local prejudice. Nor do we think our notions of equality of opportunity have much to learn from the caste societies of the Indian sub-continent. Nor are we commonly going in search of many lessons about the decent treatment of women, and of political prisoners, from the Chinese. Indeed, we hardly need to pose these questions theoretically before practice tells us the answer: millions of outsiders are beating on our doors trying to get in, and there is no reverse traffic. The strange unreality of the doctrine that all cultures are equal thus resembles the way in which Marxist moonshine used to persuade simple intellectuals in Europe that Communist states were the way of the future, when the actual inhabitants of those countries were banging on their prison walls trying to get out and into a bit of decent capitalist law and order. Political reality is indeed rather mysterious stuff, but the quickest way to discover the lie of the land is to look at where the refugees are coming from, and where they are going to.

It followed from multiculturalism that diversity of cultural composition was an unalloyed blessing for Britain, and that any doubt about this could only result from evil sentiments such as racism and xenophobia. And it was this doctrine that rapidly led to the emergence of a large and expensive bureaucracy whose point was to guarantee that migrants should share equally in the benefits of British nationality. Before long the Commission for Racial Equality (CRE) was generating antidiscrimination officers, equal opportunity consultants, tribunals, political correctness rules and other devices for enforcing on Britain the virtue of tolerance. The irony was that this virtue in its modern form was nothing but a rather strange codification of a practice whose provenance was to be found only in British (and to some extent wider European) history. Its main character was individual equality before the law. Commentators often think our tolerance inferior to that accorded to Jews and Christians in Umayyed Spain and the Ottoman Empire. These were indeed highly civilised practices, and certainly preferable to what was going on in Europe at various times. Nonetheless, the status of a *dhimmi* (one who is tolerated and taxed) in Islamic societies is not at all the same as one who enjoys equal rights in Britain.

The cutting edge of multiculturalism however is to be found in its insistence that the Anglo-Saxons and Celts of Britain must not think their language, religion, laws and customs in any way superior to those of the people who, for some mysterious reason, want to come and live here rather than stay home. The implication has in practice been that in any conflict between the migrants and local custom, local custom should give way. The migrants have had to be supplied with official materials in their own languages rather than being required to understand English; religious holidays of the new cultures have had to be accommodated by employers, and legislation had to be adapted to migrant customs. A law to enforce the wearing of crash helmets by riders on motor cycles had to be modified to accommodate Sikh practices, as did another law about the possession of knives.

It is this aspect of multiculturalism that most grates upon the average Briton, who resents the idea that whatever in the way we live any ethnic group might find *offensive* must be changed. One result of multiculturalism was that schools with an ethnic intake began to exclude Christmas festivities, including Jesus in his crib surrounded by wise men, while sundry local authorities banned the term 'Christmas' from their seasonal cards and replaced it with anodyne words, such as (in Birmingham) something called 'Winterval'. The primary school child who came home having picked up from his teacher the idea that the police were all something called 'racist' may not be entirely standard, but he does typify the kind of muddle emerging from this strange passion for attitudinal engineering. And these are relatively familiar examples of multicultural enthusiasm, because they reveal the basic level at which the doctrine irradiates British life, namely, among schoolteachers and local officials. Admittedly, the dictatorship of multicultural virtue could not operate without higher agencies such as the CRE, but at this level one often finds rather more sophistication than further down the administrative chain. Indeed, Trevor Phillips, who currently heads that Commission, has been critical of some aspects of multiculturalism in recent times.

For the remarkable thing is that the British have a lot less trouble accommodating peoples of other faiths and cultures than they have in tolerating their own home-grown multiculturalists. These local enthusiasts are way ahead of the spokesmen for ethnic minorities in discovering possible sources of ethnic offence, forever sniffing out racism and xenophobia among the natives. It is these people rather than actual immigrants who continually describe Britain as a 'racist society' and make a big play with the marvellously muddled idea of 'institutional racism'. It is notable that earlier waves of migration to Britain—Jews from the late nineteenth century, Poles before and after the Second World War—settled into British life very successfully, no doubt in part because they were not forever being told how much their sensibilities were being offended by vile local xeno-phobes. That settling in cannot have been easy—but no settling in ever is.

The human problem is that nobody much likes foreigners as such. It is much nicer to live among your own kind, people you can recognise and trust. No doubt this kind of response is unsophisticated, but the human world constantly illustrates the dislike of one group for another. Tamil and Sri Lankan, Muslim and Hindu in India, Catholic and Protestant in Northern Ireland—these may be cited merely to remind us how universal is the incidence of antipathy and conflict, and there is no country in which such ethnic passions are not found. Migration is not an adventure for the weak. The remarkable thing about Britain, and other European countries, is how easily (all things considered) it has so far been.

The eagerness of the multicultural establishment to abandon British customs, however, is one of the facts that reveals the extent to which multiculturalism arises less from love of others than from hatred of our own form of life. No other culture is ready to abandon its own convictions with the same insouciance, and the reasons for that can only be guessed at; the reasons are certainly buried deep in the nature of our civilisation. But part of it is our Western capacity for becoming so bewitched by the ideal that we learn to hate the real.

Promotion and visibility are particularly areas where multiculturalism has created the most mayhem. Senior positions in European life are a scarce resource for which people compete, usually on the basis of ability. Multiculturalism is in this context the demand that ethnic minorities should be 'represented' in senior positions in proportion to their numbers in the society at large. The dread word 'quotas' is not commonly used, but that is what it amounts to. The only way of making sense of this demand is to assume that all cultures and populations are, statistically speaking, equally good at the whole range of skills that modern Western society has generated. The implication is that wherever seniority is 'hideously white' (as a BBC Director General once put it) the cause must lie in racism and xenophobia. Again, we have a case where an impossible ideal generates Western self-scourging. It reveals how prejudiced and bad we are.

But as with the parallel case of feminism, which also drives promotion away from ability towards quotas as the test of advancement, water is being asked to run uphill. I do not know the reason, but there is no doubt that some cultures tend to specialise in some activities rather than others. No doubt such specialisations change over time— Jews who once specialised in chess and commerce, for example, turned out to be highly effective soldiers in Israel. It requires a different temperament to be a soldier from that which fits someone for nursing. This is an area where anyone sensible will be sensitive to opportunity and contingency. The last thing a society needs is a dogma to which we ˙are all bound, generating, as it inevitably does, that special kind of incompetence found in international organisations where the jobs must be shared out equally between the nations who belong to it. But one inevitable consequence of multiculturalism is a constant drip of complaint from would-be ethnic high-flyers that they are not getting a chance in law, or academia, or wherever the gravy train happens to be.

Multiculturalism might just be tolerable if it were simply a mobilisation of British decency and tolerance in favour of supposedly vulnerable people understood less as migrants than as guests to whom we owed a duty of hospitality. But the fact that it has generated an expensive and intrusive bureaucracy to dominate our lives shows that it is something different, something in fact quite alien to the historical traditions of acceptance of others that developed in Britain over hundreds of years. It has clamped onto us a dictatorship of virtue whose like has not been seen since Cromwell's major generals took us over. Its effect has been to create in Britain a corporate state, in which the government presides over a set of corporations constituted of politically correct categories. An actual vote means less and less in Britain, but the voice of these corporations is increasingly heard in the land, and its tones are becoming increasingly inescapable.

1

Don't Respect Difference: Ignore Difference

Cultural relativism, the philosophy that no culture is superior to another, is one of today's widely accepted doctrines. In the twenty-first century, to assert the superiority of Western civilisation over any other culture elicits accusations of eurocentricism, arrogance or even racism. 'All cultures are equal' is a now a commonly-heard mantra. The manifestation of cultural relativism in social policy, multiculturalism, is ubiquitous. We are persistently exhorted to 'celebrate difference' and ethnic diversity in countless fields—politics, academia, museums, films, television and literature. A Department of Trade and Industry report of 2002 summarised this dogma: 'We want to see a Britain where there is increasing empowerment; where attitudes and biases that hinder the progress of individuals and groups are tackled; where cultural, racial, and social diversity are respected and celebrated.'[1] If these words seem familiar, it is because you have most likely read them in similar form on countless occasions—at your local library, on local government leaflets, job applications—or heard them parroted by politicians over the last 40 years. Multiculturalism is one of the most resilient orthodoxies of our times.

It has also become one of the most contested issues of our times. Since its emergence as a doctrine of social policy in the 1960s, multiculturalism has had the capacity to arouse strong emotions from its apologists and detractors alike. Its apologists contend that it is imperative that we should 'celebrate difference', that it is vital for the health and well-being of a liberal society to embrace a 'live-and-let-live' attitude that accepts and embraces the value of difference. Multiculturalism is perceived as the greatest safeguard against cultural

1

conformity that leads to racism, fascism and totalitarianism. Thus, we are commanded never to be 'judgmental'. Judgmentalism is not only derided as oppressive and offensive; it is deemed to be philosophically untenable. Because all cultures have different standards, and no culture is superior or inferior to another, it is impossible to say what is truly right and what is wrong.

Conversely, multiculturalism's critics have argued that it has been a malevolent force, that its promotion has been divisive. They maintain that state-sponsored multiculturalism patronises ethnic minorities, that it has pitted ethnic groups against each other, that it has unfairly denigrated the culture of the indigenous population, and, ironically, actually served to exacerbate racism. This book is in broad agreement with the second camp. *The Poverty of Multiculturalism* argues that state-sanctioned multiculturalism has indeed been counter-productive and worsened race relations. It contends that cultural relativism, its philosophical parent, is self-contradictory: cultural relativism is an invention of the West, and thus it is self-invalidating. To promote multiculturalism is, paradoxically, to champion Western values.

The Poverty of Multiculturalism argues that this veneration of non-Western cultures is the symptom of a growing disenchantment with our own values, and even of a form of self-hatred. It is time that we respected our own culture, both as Westerners and Britons. Western culture has a rich and admirable tradition of social liberalism that says that one should be rendered as much freedom as possible in the private sphere, that one should dress according to one's desires, worship freely without molestation from the State, be afforded equal rights and participate in culturally-specific ceremonies. It is time we cherished the tradition of the Enlightenment, with its aspiration that the prizes of liberty, democracy, colour-blindness, equality of opportunity and progress can be shared among all. We should certainly afford respect to traditional British values which influenced the beneficent aspirations of the Enlightenment. While admitting our country's short-comings in the past, we should desist from perpetually dwelling on them, and recognise that of which we should be proud. Tolerance is something for which we should strive. What we might call 'Soft Multiculturalism', the idea that minorities should not face unfair discrimination and that cultures and customs of different peoples should be tolerated, is a benign force. As the broadcaster and commentator Kenan Malik has pointed out, there is a difference between multiculturalism as a lived experience and multiculturalism as an enforced ideology.[2] There is a difference between living alongside people who have different customs and outlooks, and the State encouraging us all to retain these differences, using its financial muscle to do so.

Cultural intercourse can be a healthy, fascinating and rewarding enterprise. Exploring and embracing other cultures are means of learning about our own culture's shortcomings—about what wisdom we can appropriate from 'the Other'. The study of difference, of contrasting languages, kinship structures, religions and ethnic arrangements has led us to a better understanding of the human condition in general. As Bhikhu Parekh points out in *Rethinking Multiculturalism*, a recognition of diversity leads to exchanges of ideas and philosophical enrichment: 'Different artistic, literary, musical, moral and other traditions interrogate, challenge and probe each other's ideas, and often throw up wholly new ideas and sensibilities that none of them could have generated on their own.'[3] On a pragmatic level, it is advantageous to understand how to conduct oneself elsewhere, that, for example, in India you do not use your left hand for eating, or that in Iran and Nigeria the 'thumbs-up' gesture is considered obscene, or that for Arabs, Thais and Japanese pointing the sole of your shoe at the person to whom you are talking is considered rude.

This is not to say that we can speak of cultures as monolithic entities that do not mutate, merge or appropriate aspects from each another. Neither is it to ignore the substantial shortcomings of the Western tradition, nor the achievements of non-Western cultures. What is more, *The Poverty of Multiculturalism* is not a call for the adoption of a brutal form of monoculturalism as witnessed in Nazi Germany. Most of all, this book is not principally concerned with race, even if racial and cultural categories often do overlap. Science has demonstrated to a near irrefutable degree that pigmentation is no determinant of mental ability, and that the concept of 'race' as a fixed entity is highly dubious.[4]

As opposed to race, conversely, culture does have an enormous effect on one's mental make up—and some cultures are better than others. It is true that criticism of non-Western cultures is often a cloak for racism, much in the way that anti-Israeli sentiment is often a mask for anti-semitism. But in both cases, often it is not. The very fact that any critique of another culture's shortcomings is commonly interpreted as thinly-veiled racism tells us just how far extreme multiculturalism has managed to suffocate any debate on the subject.

There is a difference between respecting different cultures and actively promoting them. The target of this book is not Soft Multiculturalism. Rather, its aim is to expose the flaws of what we might call 'Hard Multiculturalism'. This is the manifestation of cultural relativism that deems no culture better than another, which believes that a society should not merely tolerate difference, but actively promote it. We see this in evidence all around us: local and central government giving financial aid to ethnic minority groups and funding artistic projects; state schools celebrating foreign festivals and teaching the languages of ethnic minority groups; street signs in multiple languages; local libraries stocking disproportionate numbers of titles that represent the 'ethnic diversity' of its boroughs; and census returns being printed in thirteen different tongues.

This celebration of non-indigenous cultures is often accompanied by the simultaneous belittlement or vilification of British culture. History in schools concentrates not on the UK's role as a pioneer of parliamentary democracy, how it was one of the first countries to abolish slavery, how it has been a place of refuge for minorities fleeing persecution, or how it has been one of the most tolerant and peaceful nations that has ever existed. Rather, we are told to hold our heads in shame at our nation's abominable record of colonialism and oppression, the legacy of which is, today, the spectre of endemic racism in society, and 'institutional racism' in the public sphere. Multiculturalism does not mean (as it should) engaging in a spirit of mutual tolerance, while applauding assimilation; it has mutated into a philosophy of self-loathing, in which everything that is the preserve of 'the Other' has to be celebrated, and everything perceived as indigenous is regarded with indifference or contempt.

How did we get to such a state of affairs? It is partly to do with what has been dubbed the 'crisis of Britishness', in which, in a post-imperial, post-devolutionary world, the United Kingdom is no longer sure of what it stands for. Multiculturalism is a product of this vacuum. The elevation of non-indigenous cultures is both a symptom of this identity crisis and an aggravating factor: the more we have to 'celebrate diversity', the more fragmented we have become.

It is also part of a wider problem in the Western world: we live in counter-Enlightenment times. Since the Holocaust and Hiroshima, the West has lost faith in its capacity to use reason and science to make our world a better place. What with the Greenhouse Effect, the hole in the ozone layer and Chernobyl, we treat science and industry with suspicion and hostility. The failure of the socialist projects of the twentieth century led many on the

Left to give up any hope in the 'Enlightenment Project'. As the success of Michael Moore's 2002 book *Stupid White Men* illustrated, we have become self-hating, deeming Western man as an agent merely of war, racism, slavery, colonialism and environmental catastrophe. The fruits of Western society are now deemed not products of its superior values, but the results of its oppression of minority cultures. It is accepted that we grew prosperous and free and enriched the quality of our lives not because we had more progressive ideas, but because we plundered the resources of the Third World and exploited its people.

How can we possibly call ourselves superior after the carnage of the two world wars, and the cruelty of totalitarian regimes that sent millions to an early grave? We may have had the genius to split the atom, but we used that technology only to create atom bombs. We may have mostly liberated ourselves from the chimera of religion, but this has only left a spiritual void. Western society is regarded by insiders and outsiders alike as vacuous and decadent: we seem to spend our existence making money, gorging ourselves on fast food or glued to the television. Multiculturalism is a response to the perceived dreadful shortcomings of our own culture.

Because of their perverse self-loathing, many left-liberals lend their tacit or overt support to oppressive cultures that deny equal rights to its population or condone the killing of homosexuals and the virtual enslavement of women. Many exalt non-Western cultures on the understanding that they are more peaceful, 'spiritual' or 'closer to nature' than Western man, and untainted by his arrogance, brutality and greed.

This has been aggravated by and reflected in the growth of cultural relativism. Although this phenomenon was formulated by the German Romantic movement of the late eighteenth and early nineteenth centuries, it blossomed in the late twentieth century in the fields of anthropology, sociology and philosophy, and through a process of osmosis has filtered down into society in general. Just as Western man has come to hate himself, he has come to regard the culture of disenfranchised ethnic minorities as not backward or primitive, but of equal value to ours.

The contradiction is that cultural relativists sometimes want it both ways. They simultaneously assert that no culture is better than another, but they will happily elaborate that Western culture is actually inferior, and shy away from celebrating it for fear of causing 'offence'. We see this confused line of thinking in domestic social policy. While, since 1994, central and local government have been eager to use state funds to promote 'Islamic Awareness Week'—in November 2004, for instance, 50,000 copies of a package entitled *Islamophobia—Don't Suffer in Silence* were sent out to police stations, mosques and Muslim community centres in three London boroughs, West Yorkshire, Lancashire and Lincolnshire, with concomitant special lessons in state schools[5]—or fund St Patrick's Day carnivals—Birmingham City council funds such celebrations to the amount of £12,000 per year and in January 2005 promised to contribute an extra £60,000 to the celebrations[6]—these same local councils are simultaneously reluctant to celebrate Britain's Christian heritage. Indeed, they are wont to belittle it, using the excuse of 'not offending other cultures'. For instance, in 1998, Birmingham City Council—an enthusiastic supporter of Islamic Awareness Week—renamed its official Christmas celebrations 'Winterval' for fear of offending non-Christians. In November 2004 Stoke City Council followed with its 'WinterFest', as did that month Oakengates Town Council in Telford, Shropshire, with its 'Winter Celebrations'.[7] This inconsistency exposes the poverty of multiculturalism. Either public bodies should fund the celebration of Christian and Islamic faiths, or desist from spending money on celebrating either faith, but to denigrate one and venerate the other displays cognitive dissonance. Some consistency would be most welcome.

There is a more glaring paradox. Hard Multi-culturalism, as formulated by Herder and the German Romantics, and systemised by anthropologists such as Franz Boas in the 1930s, is itself a Western ideology. The notion that 'all cultures are equal' was conceived uniquely in the Euro-American school of philosophy, and is thus self-contradictory. To say 'we mustn't judge other cultures' is ironically a eurocentric statement.

Hard Multiculturalism legitimises global and domestic injustice: we are loath to criticise the oppression of women at home and abroad for fear of being admonished with the riposte: 'but that's what they do in their culture. Who are we to judge them?' Whatever the controlling section of a society does—whether it be forcing women to wear *burkhas* or stoning people to death—is deemed permissible and legitimate 'because that's how they do things there.' Hard Multiculturalism means that anything goes. It has also opened the door to irrationalism. Postmodernists have entered into an unholy alliance with Christian fundamentalists, defending their right to teach Creationism in schools, because, like evolution, it is an equally valid theory or 'discourse'.

The fruits of 30 years of state-endorsed multi-culturalism have been increased inter-racial tension and intra-racial sectarianism. Different ethnicities in the United Kingdom have grown more antagonistic towards each other, each fearing that another camp is getting a bigger slice of the financial pie than they are. In northern English cities this has not only led to increased ghettoisation between Asian and white populations, but between the Sikh, Hindu and Muslim populace. A country divided between increasingly antagonistic ethnic tribes will find it difficult to survive. The fact that the London suicide bombers of 7 July and the would-be bombers of 21 July 2005 were born and bred in Britain—and encouraged by the state to be different—illustrates that Hard Multiculturalism has the capacity to be not only divisive, but decidedly lethal.

As Samuel Huntingdon argues in his book *Who Are We? America's Great Debate* (2004), any society requires a core set of common values to function; a nation wracked by ethnic division is likely to be doomed, as Yugoslavia demonstrated. Even Hard Multiculturalists, such as Bhikhu Parekh, concede that some form of homogeneity 'facilitates a sense of community and solidarity, makes interpersonal communication easier ... is held together with relative ease, is psychologically and politically economical, and can count on and easily mobilise its members' loyalty.'[8] David Goodhart, editor of *Prospect* magazine, recently argued that this is something that should concern the Left as well as those on the Right. Goodhart, a man of impeccable left-liberal credentials, put forward the contention that a welfare state can only function when those who contribute to it feel it will be redistributed to those with whom they feel an affinity. People are reluctant to give money to those whom they do not regard as 'one of us'.[9] Unsurprisingly, even Goodhart was accused of being a racist.

Western culture has spawned the most open, liberal and progressive societies. Thanks to its Enlightenment, it has unshackled itself from oppressive and barbarous régimes, creating states in which universal franchise, free speech and democracy are the norm and the expectation.

It's time these values were cherished. It's also time to expose the poverty of multiculturalism.

2

A Brief History of Cultural Relativism

Cultural relativism is the product of the Romantic movement of the late eighteenth and early nineteenth century. Whereas Enlightenment thinkers such as Voltaire and Diderot extolled the principles of reason, justice, the brotherhood of man and of universal human rights, the Romantics sought to champion uniqueness, emotional introspection and difference. Predating the movement, but making his mark on it, was Giambattista Vico, whose views that societies' mores were incompatible influenced Johann Gottlieb Fichte and, most of all, Johann Gottfried Herder. Whereas John Stuart Mill, Locke, Hegel and Bentham contended that human nature was universal and that all human beings had the same fundamental needs and desires, the Romantics believed that human beings were principally constituted by culture, and even caged by it. From their seed has sprouted the weed of Hard Multiculturalism.

The Romantics were not the first to appreciate that human beings have different ways of doing things in different places, and that different customs should be respected. In Book III of *The Histories*, Herodotus (c.484-425 BC) posited that because we all merely obey the customs of the culture into which we are born, we must as a corollary show respect for the customs of other societies. People do things differently in foreign countries. The Greek historian recounts the first written example of culture clash in action, concerning Darius, King of the Persians: 'When he was king of Persia, he summoned the Greeks who happened to be present at his court, and asked them what they would take to eat the dead bodies of their fathers. They replied that they would not do it for any money in the world. Later, in the presence of the Greeks, and through an interpreter ... he asked some

Indians, of the tribe called Callatiae, who do in fact eat their parents' dead bodies, what they would take to burn them. They uttered a cry of horror and forbade him to mention such a dreadful thing'.[1] Similarly, the Sophists made the obvious point that men thought differently in different places. Anticipating Nietzsche's and Foucault's theory of power/knowledge, they argued that society's rulers determine what is right and wrong merely so that the ruled accept their miserable and impoverished lives as perfectly normal.

It was not until the Reformation and then the Enlightenment that the idea of cultural particularism was explored to a greater degree. In 1580 the French essayist Michel de Montaigne (1533-92) reacted to reports of widespread cannibalism in the Caribbean thus:

> I think there is nothing barbarous and savage in that nation, from what I have been told, except that each man calls barbarism whatever is not his own practice; for indeed it seems we have no other test of truth and reason than the example and pattern of the opinions and customs of the country we live in.[2]

Giambattista Vico (1688-1744) elaborated, arguing that different cultures were often incompatible. Unlike later thinkers, however, he did believe there was a thing called human nature, that mankind shared 'a common mental language'.[3] In his work of 1748, *Spirit of the Laws*, the Baron de Montesquieu (1689-1755) asserted that cultural difference was a defining and inescapable feature of human existence. His satire, the *Persian Letters* (1721), famously employed the notion of cultural dissimilarity, in which two fictional Persians visit France and observe how strange some of its customs are, such as why the Church had so much money, and why French society was so unjust and corrupt. He contrasted it unfavourably with the sincerity found in Asian countries. Nevertheless, like Vico, Montesquieu also believed man had shared desires: the capacity to employ Reason, to live among others, to seek happiness, liberty and freedom, and look after his or her family. In Montesquieu's opinion, it was external influences, such as soil and climate, which were responsible for throwing up cultural differences. In other words, they all believed that there was such a thing as human nature.

Johann Gottfried Herder (1744-1803) disagreed. He contended that man was shaped entirely by his culture, and, in particular, his language. Man can only think through words, and each language was the expression of a unique culture: 'Every nation speaks in the manner it thinks and thinks in the manner it speaks.' As Isaiah Berlin elaborated: 'Whereas Voltaire and Diderot believed that reality was ordered in terms of universal, timeless, objective, unalterable laws which rational investigation could discover, Herder maintained that every activity, situation, historical period of civilisation possessed a unique character of its own,' what Herder called a *Volksgeist*.[4]

Herder wrote that it was impossible to judge any society from the perspective of another: each culture possessed a 'singular, wonderful, inexplicable, ineradicable' identity, and its own 'spirit', 'ethos' or 'atmosphere'.[5] He shared much with today's Hard Multiculturalists: he celebrated the *Kultur* of the *Volk* in opposition to the *Zivilisation* of the city. What he detested more than anything else was 'the assimilation of one culture by another.' There is here the almost mystical veneration of culture for its own sake, an appeal to the aesthetic: the failure to grasp that cultures are not hermetically sealed, organic wholes, or the recognition that they contain tensions, or that they evolve and mutate. Herder and disciples such as Johann Gottlieb Fichte (1762-1814) systemised the philosophy of ethnic particularism, which has inspired both Nazism and Hard Multiculturalism. If this appears paradoxical, then one has to recognise that both ideologies are hostile to the values of the Enlightenment; to both, preserving the essence of cultures against universalising tendencies is of primary concern.

Nor is it a coincidence that the ideas of Friedrich Nietzsche (1844-1900) were appropriated by both camps. While Herder was possessed principally of an aesthetic mindset that revered difference, Nietzsche's invectives made an epistemological assault on the Judeo-Christian mindset and the concept of truth. Works such as *The Genealogy of Morals* (1887) and *Beyond Good and Evil* (1888) sought to expose the fallacy of conventional moralities, asserting that our concepts of right and wrong are designed by individuals and groups in order to suit their particular needs. Aristocrats at the top of society believed in the divine order of things because this convinces the masses that their rightful place is at the bottom. Socialists believe in the redistribution of wealth only because they are poor and envious. Philosophers only create systems of thought to justify their own ethical prejudices. What we hold to be good and evil, right and wrong, is nothing but a product of a Will To Power. God was dead, and so was our source of morality. And, as Dostoevsky said, if there is no God, everything is permitted.

Nietzsche, like Paul Valery and Oswald Spengler, perceived there to be something rotten and decadent at the heart of Western civilisation: he believed that it had become weak, complacent and obsessed with material goods. This sentiment was developed in the twentieth century, when, in the words of John Lukacs:

> the appeal of the cult of Reason, of the applications of Progress, and the usage of 'modern' itself began to weaken, not only among intellectuals but among more and more people.[6]

The corollary of increased self-loathing and self-doubt, which Freud's *Civilization and its Discontents* (1930) investigated, was a burgeoning interest in that which was non-Western. From the 1920s onwards social anthropologists sought to understand non-Western cultures on their own terms, not from the values of the observer. At Columbia University, Franz Boas (1858-1942) did make a commendable breakthrough in his findings that there is no such thing as racial purity, but he also concluded that no ethnic group is innately superior to another. On the other side of the Atlantic, A. J. Ayer in *Language, Truth and Logic* (1936) claimed that the language of morality was meaningless. Those who say that 'murder is wrong' are merely expressing their feelings, they are merely expressing the personal opinion that they find killing someone without justification distasteful.

By the 1960s, the notion that societies can be judged superior or inferior to each other was finding little favour.[7] Right and wrong are determined by culture; there is no universal, objective, truth—only particular, subjective, interpretation. Michel Foucault (1926-84), after Nietzsche, declared that power is knowledge. It is the wielders of authority who determine what is true or not. As Foucault put it:

> Knowledge is simply the outcome of the interplay, the encounter, the junction, the struggle and the compromise between the instincts. Something is produced because the instincts meet, fight one another, and at the end of their battles finally reach a compromise. That something is knowledge.[8]

According to the prominent epistemologist Trevor Pinch of Cornell University:

> What makes a belief true is not its correspondence with an element of reality, but its adoption and authentications by the relevant community.[9]

The philosopher Richard Rorty has echoed these sentiments: 'truth is what your contemporaries let you get away with.'[10]

Saussurean linguistics and Jacques Lacan's exposition of the fiction of 'the self' told us that our mind, and our concept of the world, is shaped solely by our language, and, elaborating, Jacques Derrida proclaimed that even the meaning of words is unstable, and thus truth is unknowable. If there is no way of knowing what is 'out there', then it is surely impossible for any culture to proclaim privileged access to truth. So let's celebrate difference. In 1971 two noted anthropologists, Catherine

H. Berndt and Ronald M. Berndt, expressed this relativist doctrine thus:

> In serious comparative studies, 'savage' and 'barbarian', with its 'barbarous' overtones, are no longer acceptable as labels for categories of mankind ... There is something altogether too derogatory about them, too obviously ethnocentric.[11]

Anthropology and the humanities in general have not altered this semantic stance since. 'Cultures are comparable but not commensurable; each is what it is, of literally inestimable value in its own society, and consequently to humanity as a whole' asserted Isaiah Berlin[12]. Or more stridently put: 'Each human culture is so unique', insists the anthropologist Renato Rosaldo: '[n]o one of them is higher or lower, greater or lesser than any other.'[13]

Today we have reached the stage where 'culture' has been essentialised, and specific cultures perceived almost as quasi-biological entities. They are regarded as akin to endangered species or threatened rainforests, as precious organic entities that must be cherished, respected and protected at all costs. There is evidently an aesthetic appeal to protecting them, of course. 'Wouldn't the world be a boring place if we were all the same?' is a commonplace argument. 'Why should we take the diversity of human cultures less seriously than the diversity of animal or plant species?' asks the Lebanese cultural critic, Amin Maalouf.[14]

Nonetheless, this sentiment veers dangerously close to an almost racist appreciation of mankind, which dictates that we belong to mutually exclusive groups, almost as if we are of different species. It mirrors the French philosopher Joseph de Maistre's remark, that while he had met a Frenchman, an Italian and a Russian, 'as for man, I declare that I have never in my life met him; if he exists he is unknown to me.'

3

Civilisation and Its Malcontents

The 'celebration' of non-Western cultures is the symptom of a mood of suspicion about Western achievements, a suspicion that borders on hostility. As one commentator remarked after the 9/11 attacks, the question is not to ask 'Why do they hate us so much?', but 'Why do we hate ourselves so much?'[1] We are witnessing the revolt of the civilised against civilisation.

Many appear to concur with James Lovelock's Gaia theory, that man—especially Western man—is a plague on the planet. The progressive optimism of the nineteenth century has been eroded by the experience of two world wars, and in increasing numbers and increasing intensity, Westerners are prone to regard the Enlightenment as a ghastly mistake. Its political programme for equality and justice is damned as merely spawning the murderous Marxist and Nazi regimes of the twentieth century, which were morally bankrupt, politically oppressive, and economically and ecologically catastrophic. Before their eventual collapse at the end of the century, communist régimes sent an estimated 80 million souls to an early grave. The only alternative, Western capitalism, is derided as selfish, or accepted with a foreboding sense of guilt. It is unsurprising that the vast majority of relativists are formerly of the rationalist Left, seeing the Enlightenment as a hopeless and disastrous disappointment.

'The worst régimes of the twentieth century were shaped—largely or in part—by Enlightenment ideas', writes the philosopher and writer John Gray, one of the most prominent anti-Enlightenment figures in Britain.[2] The Holocaust is regarded not as an aberration of modernity, but, according to the philosopher Zygmunt

Bauman, as its logical consequence: it was the result of the desire of Enlightenment Man to classify, rationalise, and separate civilised man from uncivilised man: 'Every ingredient of the Holocaust ... was normal ... in the sense of being fully in keeping with everything we know about our civilisation, its guiding spirits, its priorities, its immanent vision of the world—and of the proper ways to pursue human happiness together with a perfect society'.[3]

The trust we had in science has also been corroded. Although its advances have helped us to live longer, healthier lives—most of us can look forward to dying in our sleep at an old age—many seem convinced that science is actually a malign force. Scientists are no longer people to look up to and admire, but to fear, through their unchecked 'arrogance', whether this be human cloning or genetically-modified 'Frankenstein foods'. Nuclear energy is no longer regarded as the panacea, but, after the Chernobyl disaster in particular, as a pestilence. Acid rain, the Greenhouse Effect, the depletion of the ozone layer and the Brazilian rainforests: all are perceived either as the consequence of placing our misguided faith in science, or of our rapacious thirst for more consumer goods. Today the word 'civilisation' is seldom written without those contemptuous inverted commas, implying that either we in the West are not civilised at all, or that the whole notion of 'civilisation' was a dangerous concept in the first place. Echoing Susan Sontag's belief that 'the white race is the cancer of human history', former Labour MP Tony Banks summed up this self-loathing when in early 2004 he proposed a motion in Parliament that included the statement: 'This House ... believes that humans represent the most obscene, perverted, cruel, uncivilised and lethal species ever to inhabit the planet, and looks forward to the day when the inevitable asteroid slams into the Earth and wipes them out thus giving Nature the opportunity to start again.'[4]

This popular mood of anti-modernist anti-humanism is a modern day version of romanticism that is fond of finding faults with much that is 'Western' and rational. In the words of the anti-Enlightenment philosopher David Goldberg:

> Subjugation defines the order of the Enlightenment: subjugation of nature by human intellect, colonial control through physical and cultural domination, and economic superiority through mastery of the laws of the market.[5]

'The universalising discourses of modern Europe and the United States', Edward Said elaborated, 'assume the silence, willing or otherwise, of the non-European world.'[6]

This climate of self-hatred can be witnessed at street level by the popularity of the American film-maker and author Michael Moore. As he maintains in his *Stupid White Men*:

> I look around at the world I live in ... it's not the African-Americans who have made this planet such a pitiful, scary place ... No black guy ever built or used a bomb designed to wipe out hordes of innocent people, whether in Oklahoma City, Columbine or Hiroshima. No friends, it's always the white guy.[7]

From popular musings such as Moore's to sentiments often expressed in academe, the message is the same: 'anything and everything done in or by some non-Western culture [is] good or at least neutral', observed one eminent anthropologist, while 'everything done in or by Western society is seen as bad.'[8] Western man (especially of the white variety) beats his breast today, denouncing himself as 'unwittingly racist', sporting metaphorical sackcloth and ashes to apologise for crimes of the past.

The urge to improve the lot of non-Europeans is now seen as a cover for naked imperialism, which resulted in the oppression of peoples around the globe and the attempted extermination of their cultures. Christopher Columbus is now viewed as a villain. 'Columbus makes Hitler look like a juvenile delinquent,' stated Russell Means, a leader of the American Indian Movement in

1989. He said that asking Native Americans to celebrate Columbus Day was akin to asking Jews to take a 'balanced view of the Holocaust' on Hitler Day.[9] In the process, there has emerged a tendency to elevate non-Western lifestyles, be they past or present. The revolt of the civilised against civilisation is not a new phenomenon, as we have seen. Romantic primitivism, that Western weakness for loathing one's own advanced civilisation, and wishing one lived among simpler, more exotic folk, dates back to Classical Greece, with the Cynics and the Stoics. Montaigne cherished the exotic lifestyles of the indigenous peoples of the Caribbean; Jean-Jacques Rousseau despaired that European civilisation had enchained us all, removing us from our free and peaceful (and mythical) state of nature; the anthropologist Margaret Mead wrote a romantic and engaging account of *Coming of Age in Samoa* (1928), in which she lavished praise on its inhabitants' practice of free love (an account that was subsequently spectacularly discredited).

Romantic primitivism has experienced a renaissance in recent decades as a reaction to the faults perceived as inherent in the Western vision. As the eco-activist Stephanie Mills, the editor of *Turning Away from Technology: A New Vision for the 21st Century* (1997), asserts: 'As a species, human beings have more experience living wild, in hunter-gatherer bands, embedded in healthy ecosystems.' The writer Anne Pederson agrees: 'Ancient people knew that they depended on the natural world for survival and had a close relationship with the forces of sky and earth... The people of ancient societies did not regard the human community as separate from the world of nature. The Earth was often seen as a Mother, the giver and nourisher of life.' Kirkpatrick Sale, in *The Conquest of Paradise* (1991), concurs, maintaining that pre-Columbian Indians lived 'in balanced and fruitful harmony' with nature in 'an untouched world, a prelapsarian Eden of astonishing plenitude'.[10] In films such as Kevin Costner's *Dances with Wolves* (1990), the accepted norms of the

Hollywood Western were inverted, so that it is the white man who is the brutal savage, and the Indians the custodians of culture and civility—a people that seems, in the words of one unsympathetic reviewer, to be 'a mix of Timotei models and Relate therapists'.[11] The West has been lost. Disney's *Pocahontas* (1995) echoed this sentiment, portraying the British as the barbarians, and the indigenous Indians as saintly and serene. In *Earth in the Balance* (1992), Al Gore lamented that we in the West had erected a false world of 'plastic flowers and Astroturf, air conditioning and fluorescent lights, windows that do not open and music that never stops, sleepy hearts jumpstarted by caffeine, alcohol, drugs and illusions'.[12] Or as Joni Mitchell once sang: 'They paved paradise/ and put up a parking lot.' Many people still seem to agree that it would be preferable if we all returned to a state of harmony with nature (one that never existed).

This self-belittlement of Western man's achievements has been accompanied at home by what has been called 'the crisis of Britishness'. We partly romanticise 'the Other' because we are not so sure what 'the Self' is anymore. As has been argued in Linda Colley's *Britons* (1992), Richard Weight's *Patriots* (2002) (and elsewhere in works by Andrew Marr, Peter Hitchens, Tom Nairn and Simon Heffer) British identity was traditionally underpinned by two central concepts: Protestantism and Empire. Now that Britain is no longer really a Protestant nation and the Empire a thing of the past, a sense of Britishness is disintegrating, spawning an increase in the desire by the Scots and the Welsh to leave the Union, which has in turn led to a growing mood of English nationalism. For instance, when England won the World Cup in 1966, the crowd at Wembley Stadium could be seen waving Union Flags; 30 years later at the European Championships, it had been entirely displaced by the St George Cross. According to a Mori poll of 2000, only 18 per cent of Scots, 27 per cent of Welsh and 43 per cent of English describe themselves as British.[13]

This development has been accompanied by much soul searching among the English, who unlike their neighbours north and west of the border, do not have obvious cultural signifiers of ethnic particularity. Scotland has its tartan, its kilts and its bagpipes; Wales has its language, its singing, its Methodism and its rugby. England has no obvious equivalent. Thus, there has been much tortured debate since the mid-1990s about what it actually means to be British and English. Even so, and while the term 'British' is now usually used as a term of self-description by people from ethnic minorities, it remains simultaneously derided. In October 2000, a report from the Commission on the Future of Multi-Ethnic Britain, asserted that 'Britishness' was an alien concept for some citizens of the UK as it had 'systematic, largely unspoken, racial connotations'.[14]

Post-Enlightenment and Post-British feelings are characterised by the same temptation: to deride one's own culture and, to fill the void, to venerate non-Western, non-British cultures. It is a potent compound that has opened the door for the return of irrationalism.

4

The New Irrationalism

Cultural relativism is not only politically divisive, but it legitimises irrationality and superstition. Any sort of nonsense can be afforded credibility today under the banner of cultural relativism, with its opponents branded 'offensive' or 'racist'.

Through her book *Evolution as Religion* (1985), Mary Midgley popularised the notion that science is a kind of faith, and that evolution is our modern original myth. We turn to it to explain why we are here, what is good and evil. Science does not contain eternal truths; it is shaped by who is practising it and by the concerns of the culture from which it springs. After Nietzsche, who argued that truth is merely the solidification of old metaphors,[1] and Derrida's theory of deconstruction, in which words are deemed not to refer to outside reality, science is no longer deemed to contain logical coherence and be able to discover any concrete truths. Consequently, the claims of Western science must be treated with suspicion. 'Western science is only a culturally specific form of ethnoscience, not a universally valid way of verification or falsification', asserts one noted anthropologist.[2]

At a 1996 meeting of the American Association for the Advancement of Science, radical feminists, blacks and others made the contention that science is merely a means through which white men have asserted their dominance in Western society. The assault on reason in the classroom under the banner of multiculturalism has been particularly acute in the United States. A 1996 journal article published in the US for mathematics teachers asserted that the reason why some Navajo schoolchildren were failing at the subject was that 'the Western world developed the notion of fractions and decimals out of need to divide or segment a whole. The Navajo world view consistently appears not to segment the whole of the entity.'[3] Teachers of Navajo children were encouraged to deal with concepts more 'naturally compatible with Navajo spatial knowledge' such as 'non-Euclidean geometry, motion theories, and/or fundamentals of calculus'.[4] The idea that one can teach calculus before fractions is ridiculous, and such perverse pedagogy does a profound disservice to pupils. There has concomitantly emerged the move to promote 'ethnomathematics'. In 1996, the International Study Group on Ethnomathematics released a paper in the USA calling for the promotion of 'multicultural mathematics'. It asserted that all talk of being 'good' or 'bad' at the discipline was a nonsense, ridiculing the 'so-called Pythagorean theorem' and urging 'culturally responsive pedagogy'. By 1996, more than three quarters of teachers in the USA had implemented 'ethnomathematic' guidelines.[5]

Exasperated by this assault on science, the evolutionary biologist Richard Dawkins once asked an anthropologist the following:

> Suppose there is a tribe ... who believe that the moon is an old calabash tossed into the sky, hanging only just out of reach above the treetops. Do you really claim that our scientific truth—that the moon is about a quarter of a million miles away and a quarter of the diameter of the Earth—is no more true than the tribe's calabash? 'Yes,' the anthropologist said, 'we are just brought up in a culture that sees the world in a scientific way. They are brought up to see the world in another way. Neither way is more true than the other'.[6]

The said anthropologist's contention would not be taken seriously by most lay people, although, within the corridors of academe, it would not be ridiculed so easily. Anthropologists are not immune to the ridiculous. Martha Nussbaum wrote that once she attended a conference at which a French anthropologist gave a paper in which he argued that the elimination of smallpox in India was regrettable, as it had also 'eradicated the cult of Sittala

Devi, the goddess to whom one used to pray in order to avert smallpox'. Far from being a welcome move, the introduction of the vaccine, the anthropologist insisted, was merely 'another example of Western neglect of difference'. When the objection was made 'that it was surely better to be healthy rather than ill, to live rather than to die', the anthropologist sighed that this was just typical Western thinking, 'which conceives of things in terms of binary oppositions'.[7]

There are signs that cultural relativism is facilitating an alarming development: the assertion, in the teaching of Creationism in its extreme form that the world was created 6,000 years ago (or, more precisely, at 9 a.m. on the morning of Sunday, 23 October 4004 BC, as the seventeenth-century biblical critic John Lightfoot calculated). In 1999 the state of Kansas agreed to remove the teaching of Darwinist evolution from its state schools. Emmanuel College in Gateshead, north-east England, indoctrinates its pupils with Creationist myths, while a Seventh-Day Adventist School in Tottenham, North London, has been doing likewise, at the taxpayers' expense, since 1998. Increasingly it is argued that, alongside evolution, Creationism is an equally valid narrative. In his book *River Out of Eden*, Richard Dawkins recalled that he seldom seemed to deliver a public lecture without a member of the audience standing up to assert: 'Fundamentally, your belief in evolution comes down to faith, and therefore it's no better than somebody else's belief in the Garden of Eden.'[8] This opinion point is not merely confined to academe: as one correspondent in the *Daily Telegraph* recently parroted: 'Creationism is no more a religion than Darwinism—or atheism for that matter. They are all beliefs; none can be proved.'[9] Nigel McQuoid, the headmaster of Emmanuel College, agreed: both creationism and evolution are 'faith positions'.[10] This is a sentiment echoed in Serbia, which recently re-instituted creationism in its school curriculum. 'Darwinism is a theory as dogmatic as the one which says God created the first man', explained its education minister, Ljilana Colic, in September 2004.[11]

The march of unreason extends beyond the classroom and the lecture hall. In February 1998 the Supreme Court of Canada accepted the claim by the Gitxsan tribe of British Columbia for the possession of 22,000 square miles of territory—on account of the tribe's belief that the territory contained the essence of a dead ancestor (who had been turned into a bear and then killed by accident).[12] In November 2002, a Maori tribe halted the construction of a multimillion dollar highway in New Zealand, protesting that it would infringe the domain of a dangerous 'swamp-dwelling monster' (known as *taniwha*) which did not care for automobiles. Unless the new road was built away from the swamp 'we're going to have more problems than what it's worth', said Maori spokesperson, Brenda Maxwell. 'They're willing to trample on our culture. Get away from the swamp. It's as simple as that.'[13] In 2004, Canadian Indians returned to the fore when scientists in British Columbia sought to return a whale to the open sea. The animal had taken to swimming close to the shore, where it had become a danger to itself and shipping, but indigenous Indians successfully protested that the whale was in fact a dead tribal leader who had returned in mutated form. In Britain in 2001, a court ruled that a shopkeeper in Soho, London, could be allowed to appoint a *feng shui* expert to decide whether his landlord could relocate him to other premises.[14]

The Chief of the Western Mohegans, Sachem Golden Eagle, managed in 2003 to sue the governor of New York state for 200 years of backdated rent, insisting that he and the state legislators were trespassing on his tribe's territory every time they went to work. He also persuaded a federal judge to stop construction of a $5m park project, claiming the government was building on sacred ground. Sachem Golden Eagle was also exposed in June 2004 as an impostor, his real name being the decidedly Waspish-sounding Ronald Roberts. He had made up the tribe of the 'Western Mohegans' and had invented his ethnic identity to carry out such schemes, which included successfully persuading Chicago investors to give him $900,000 to build a casino.[15]

The logical response to those who assert that the world was created 6,000 years ago is: 'no it wasn't'. To those who protest that there are swamp monsters and tribal elders disguised as whales, it should be said: 'no there aren't'. It is one thing to believe something in private, and freedom of religion is a cornerstone of Western civilisation, but it is another to have public policy and court judgments influenced by mumbo-jumbo.

5

Rethinking 'The Others'

The idea that no culture is better or worse than another ignores the reality of the human condition: that some societies are tyrannical, oppressive, violent, that they inflict pain on their members and deny them basic freedoms; while others are open, democratic, peaceable, permitting freedom of speech and of association. It is true that the West has an ambiguous record in this respect, but it is precisely because it has had the capacity for open introspection and the capacity to improve itself, that more open and free societies are found in the West than elsewhere in the world today. An English Jew in 2005 enjoys a far better living than his co-religionists did under the anti-semitic reign of Edward I. A Frenchman today inhabits a better country than his compatriots did under the Terror of the 1790s. Show me a cultural relativist living in Germany today who believes that his country's society in the 1930s was 'no worse, no better' than today, and I'll show you a liar. Oppression, terror and physical pain are not mere 'discourses' but real experiences.

Hard Multiculturalism is a Western indulgence for a people who have never had to suffer state- or communally-sanctioned brutality. As Roger Sandall's *The Culture Cult* and Robert Whelan's *Wild in Woods: The Myth of the Noble Eco-Savage* have persuasively argued, the idea that non-Western or primitive societies are peaceful and 'respect nature' is a persistent Western conceit. Small scale, pre-agricultural, non-literate societies are invariably characterised by a strict sense of conformity and often extreme cruelty.[1] The idea that non-urban societies are peaceful semi-paradises goes back to Aristophanes, Tacitus and the Old Testament, but it has always been a myth.

Even the Rousseauian Eric Fromm, in his *The Anatomy of Human Destructiveness*, which postulates that pre-modern man was not essentially violent, cannot refute the argument that pre-agricultural societies are not harmonious utopias. Citing 'the most peaceful tribes', such as the Zuni Indians from the southwest of the present day United States, Fromm concedes that they had squabbles over sheep raising, that their society contained much sexual jealousy, and that boys were whipped as a form of chastisement.[2] The worst form of primitive society, he concluded, was that found among the Dobu Islanders, in which relationships between husbands and wives were characterised by mutual suspicion. As far as non-sexual relationships were concerned: 'All existence is cut-throat competition and every advantage is gained at the expense of the defeated rival. But competition is not, as in other systems, open and frank, but secret and treacherous. The ideal of a good and successful man is one who has cheated another of his place.' It is a society in which those who seek to murder a competitor feign to befriend him beforehand to lower his defences. As one Dobu Islander told an anthropologist: 'If we wish to kill a man we approach him, we eat, drink, sleep, work and rest with him, it may be for several moons. We bide our time. We call him friend.'[3]

The savagery found in primitive societies is well documented. Consider the custom of peoples of highland New Guinea, described in Robert B. Edgerton's book *Sick Societies*. Before contact with white Australians, most 'societies throughout highland Papua New Guinea ... required that boys go through initiation ceremonies in which they were forced to drink only partly slaked lime that blistered their mouths and throats, were beaten with stinging nettles, were denied water, had barbed grass pushed up their urethras to cause bleeding, were compelled to swallow bent lengths of cane until vomiting was induced, to fellate older men, who also had anal intercourse with them.' Reports by reliable witnesses relate that the climate at that time was not one of acquiescence, but one of fear and terror.[4]

Practices carried out in many non-Western cultures, past and present, are renowned for their brutality. The ancient Spartans institutionalised pederasty, encouraged their youth to murder neighbouring Messanians and practised euthanasia, in which unwanted, sickly or deformed babies were hurled to their deaths down a ravine. The rearing of children was for the express purpose of transforming them into soldiers. They were given few clothes, were poorly-fed, slept on bare ground, were encouraged to steal to supplement their rations, tell lies, fight each other and go on expeditions to terrify Messanian slaves.[5] Far from being peaceful farmers, as is the popular perception, indigenous Indians in what is now Colorado practised periodic and then routine cannibalism from 900 AD to 1150 AD,[6] as did the pre-conquest Maoris and Aztecs. According to archaeologists, the Chinese of c.500,000 BC used to eat each other's brains, while infanticide was widespread in Canaan at the time of the Hebrew conquest, as it was in Carthage up until the Roman conquest in the third century BC.[7] To this day, cannibalism is still practised among tribes in Borneo and Papua New Guinea.[8]

In the case of the Aztecs, the victim was often a prisoner of war or a slave who was forced back by a priest on a sacrificial stone. The victim's breast was cut open with a flint knife, his heart torn out and burnt in a stone urn. Other ceremonies included drowning, decapitation or burning. Mary Midgley has explored the custom in medieval Japan called *tsujirgiri*, in which Samurai could legitimately test their swords on passers-by in the road, in which they sought to cut the unfortunates in half.[9]

It would be ahistorical to condemn such practises as mindlessly barbaric. Such customs appeared logical in the eyes of their protagonists at the time. Pressure for land in ancient Sparta was intense, and euthanasia was a response to the feared perils of overpopulation. The

Spartans also had a strong military code and believed that their youth needed to be reared as fearless in preparation for war. And, thanks to its rigid military code, Sparta became the most powerful city state in Greece, eventually triumphing over Athens in the Peloponnesian War (431-404 BC). Samurai warriors also had a strict code of honour. If, in battle, they failed to cut their enemies in half with one stroke, they and their lord would be shamed. The practice of attacking strangers was thus, for them, necessary practise. The Aztecs believed that human sacrifice was a sacred duty to their gods and feared that, should they not undertake it, the deities would be angered and render their land infertile. To the victims, it was not all bad, either. Death by sacrifice was understood to guarantee a happy afterlife. Yet, to defend behaviour because its actors believe in its authenticity is to defend irrationalism, superstition and theocracy.

Racism and ethnocentricity, casually understood by many as essentially Western inventions, are not unknown to other societies. Contrarily, ethnocentrism has always been the norm of humanity. It is an adaptive trait that has helped to secure the propagation of peoples. Differing groups of Australian Aboriginals are highly ethnocentric. In many instances, a people's name for themselves is translatable as 'human being', rendering other tribes 'non-humans'. A tribe of north-eastern Australia called the 'Arnhem Landers' mocks the unintelligible 'bird-speech' of its neighbours to the south, and consider them so beyond the pale of normality that it used go on head-hunting tours of them.[10] Historians of the Han dynasty in the third century BC recall their encounters with savages 'who greatly resemble the monkeys from whom they are descended'. The invading Aryans of ancient India described themselves as 'nobly born', comparing themselves favourably to the dark-skinner natives they called Anaryan or *dasa* (slave). The Zulus compared members of rival tribes to animals. Muslim travellers in the Middle Ages were given to making derogatory comments about non-Muslim blacks, with one eleventh-century scholar describing the Ethiopians and Nubians as 'fickle, foolish, ignorant and lacking in self-control'. Muslims of the time had little time for white non-Muslim Europeans, either. The Muslim writer Sai'd al-Andalusi wrote of the Slavs that 'their temperaments are frigid, their humours raw ... they lack keenness of understanding and clarity of intelligence, and are overcome by ignorance and dullness, lack of discernment and stupidity'.[11] These comments may be regarded as culturalist rather than racist, as Muslim writers of the period poured scorn on Europeans and black Africans, not because of their race, but rather because they were not Muslims and thus uncivilised. In this regard their viewpoint may be seen as legitimate, in that Islamic civilisation was, in many respects, superior to Christian Europe's at this time.

Male subjugation of women has also been a universal trait of humankind, and not the preserve of Western man. Men have approved of wife-beating in virtually every primitive society.[12] The practice of sending widows to the grave with their deceased husbands has not been confined to India: it was once common in China, parts of Africa, ancient Greece, Scandinavia and Russia.[13]

While the West is unique in being the first society to abolish slavery, the phenomenon of slavery has been universal. It was practised in ancient Mesopotamia, India and China, among the Aztecs, Incans and the Mayans; in Greece and Rome; and among Islamic states. American Indians were not the noble savages that Kevin Costner would have us believe. Prior to European settlement, for example, slaves comprised between 10 and 15 per cent of the population of the Americas.[14] The Lakota tribe, portrayed so sympathetically in Dances with Wolves (1990), stole land from the neighbouring Pawnee tribe, and customarily murdered the wives of the Pawnee warriors they had slain.[15] Not that the Pawnee were angels: to appease their gods, they sacrificed children, torturing them before the infants met their grisly end.[16] In 1807, the year in which the slave trade was abolished in Britain (it being the second country, after Denmark, to do so), there were more slaves in Africa than in the entire Americas. 'The slave trade has been the ruling principle of my people,' declared King Gezo of Dahomey in 1840. 'It is the source of their glory and wealth.'[17] We should not just hold Europeans responsible for slavery. According to Hugh Thomas in The Slave Trade, also guilty are 'the rulers of Benin, the kings of Ashanti, Congo, and Dahomey, and Vili rulers of Loango, who sold great numbers of slaves over many generations'.[18] At the beginning of the twenty-first century, slave girls remain on sale in Sudan, Mozambique and the Ivory Coast for as little as £5 each.[19] While willing to atone for our ancestors crimes in human trafficking, we fail to condemn Africa's present-day slave trade. It is as if we are saying that we only expect humane behaviour of ourselves, a message that surely has racist undertones.

The notion that indigenous cultures 'live in harmony' with nature is also a conceit. Cold, greedy Western man is not the only variety of homo sapiens to have practised an 'unsustainable' lifestyle. Shortly after the Polynesian Maoris arrived in New Zealand in about 1200 AD, nearly 30 per cent of the country's bird life had become extinct. The populous Giant Moa bird, which was slow and carried much meat, had been hunted to extinction by 1400 AD. The extermination of all 12 of the islands' moa species in this period is understood to be the fastest megafaunal extinction the world has ever experienced. In their pursuit of moa, the Maoris chased them out of their forests by burning down the said forests, so that, by the time Captain Cook arrived in 1770, 50 per cent of the islands' forests had disappeared. The Maoris were not so kind to their fellow humans, either. In 1835, 900 Maoris from the North Island of New Zealand invaded the Chatham Islands and 'killed hundreds of Moriori, cooked and ate many of the bodies, and enslaved all the others, killing most of them too over the next few years as it suited their whim'. In accordance with the 'it's my culture excuse', one of the Maori later explained:

> Not one escaped. Some ran away from us, these were killed, and others were killed, but what of that? It was in accordance with our custom.[20]

Extreme deforestation was also a custom of the Native American Indians, who burnt down acres of trees in their pursuit of bison, moose, elk and deer. According to one authority, deforestation in the Americas was more extensive prior to European settlement than it was afterwards.[21] In one important respect pre-agricultural, pre-modern societies do live with nature—in that they are slaves to nature. Archaeologists believe that life expectancy at birth for primitive hunter-gatherers was 26 years.[22] Thanks to Western man's 'unnatural' inventions and discoveries—such as hospitals, penicillin, inoculations, heart transplants and so on—most of us can now look forward to dying in our sleep in our 80s.

This is not to call for a return to the Victorian notion that cultures should be charted teleologically, that all are on some mystical time chart, some more 'ahead' and some more 'behind'. Rather it is to urge that we retain the notion that some can be regarded as superior and some as inferior, some better and some worse. For instance, as Franz Boas revealed, the Kwakiutl tribe of North America have no linguistic difference between singular and plural: 'There is a house over there' and 'There are some houses over there' are indistinguishable. The distinction between present and past is not made in Eskimo societies ('The man is coming' *vs* 'The man was coming').[23] And the small Piraha tribe of Brazil, who live in the Lowland Amazon area, have no numeral words beyond one, two and many. Even their 'one' can mean 'a few' and 'two' is interchangeable with 'not many'.[24] Consequently, concluded Peter Gordon of Columbia University in New York, their skill levels were similar to those of prelinguistic infants, monkeys, birds and rodents. 'Primitive' is a word that should be applied to such societies.

6

Three Multicultural Paradoxes

The statement that 'All cultures are equal' raises the question: 'Who says so?' The problem with Hard Multiculturalism is that it is self-contradictory.

First of all, it is a variation of the paradox of the Cretan Liar who said 'This statement is false'. If all truth is relative, then why should we believe the person who utters the statement that all truth is relative? This is an uncomfortable 'truth' for relativists: to declare objectivity a fiction is itself an objective utterance, and thus self-defeating.

Secondly, tolerance in the name of relativism has become its own intolerance. We are commanded to respect all difference and anyone who disagrees shall be shouted down, silenced or slandered as a racist. Everyone must be tolerant. And that's an order.

Thirdly, while postmodernists deride the universalising rationalism of the Enlightenment as a European invention, they often fail to recognise that cultural relativism was also devised in the West. No other culture has emerged with the theory that all cultures are relative. Although societies through space and time have preached tolerance towards others, and spoken about the wisdom that alternative societies may bestow on their own, only from the West, from the post-Enlightenment canon, has there emerged the idea that cultures are incomparable, that no single version has access to truth.

Although Foucault, Derrida, *et al.* are seen to have broken from the Enlightenment tradition, their work drew substantially from Herder and Nietzsche, who themselves were inspired by Shakespeare and Kant, and Schopenhauer and Plato, respectively. The school of social anthropology, where one can find relativism articulated at its fiercest, also emerged in the West in the 20th century under the tutelage of Malinowski, Boas and A. R. Radcliffe-Brown, who themselves were intellectually indebted to Emile Durkheim, who in turn was influenced by Auguste Comte. Comte was himself the most strident disciple of rationalism. Cultural relativism is the bastard child of Western philosophy.

But, some might say, what about the influence of non-European relativists such as Edward Said or Homi K Bhabha? Yet, Said could not have written *Orientalism* (1978) before Foucault; and he also cites as an abiding influence Antonio Gramsci's idea of 'hegemony'. Similarly, without Foucault, we could not have had Cornel West's 'black cultural studies'; and without Heidegger there would have been no Bhabha. They are the products of the Western canon.

By their own core principle, that an idea conceived in one society cannot be applied to another, cultural relativists must insist that relativism be restricted to the European sphere. When someone pronounces, 'How do we know our culture is correct? We must respect all cultures', the answer should be: 'Don't be so eurocentric. It is unfair to preach cultural relativism. After all, it is alien to many cultures.'

Not only is Hard Multiculturalism a paradox, it ironically gives succour to that which it ostensibly seeks to eradicate: racism. The conduct of Europeans is held up to intense scrutiny, in that we are meant to feel ashamed for slavery and colonialism and apologise for the crimes of our ancestors. Yet when it comes to barbaric practices carried out in non-Western cultures, we are expected to forgive such behaviour as female circumcision and the oppression of women, because it is 'part of their culture'. In effect, we only demand civilised behaviour from Westerners, we only hold ourselves up to accountability. It is as if non-white, non-Western people are inherently backwards and—almost like children—cannot be expected to act any better.

We observed this during the 2001 war in Afghanistan. Some thought it a good thing that women in the country were no longer obliged to wear long, face-concealing *burkhas*, now that the Taliban régime had been removed. Others disagreed. The *Guardian's* Madeleine Bunting accused her arch-secularist colleague, Polly Toynbee, of promoting 'liberal fundamentalism'. In the *Independent*, Mary Dejevsky conjectured that 'the veil, whether it takes the form of a full burqa, a black chador or just a headscarf, is a cultural phenomenon that cannot just be thrown off overnight'.[1]

Somehow we regard non-Westerners as too simple to appropriate such concepts as rights, tolerance and equality. As Robert Hughes caustically observed in *The Culture of Complaint*:

> Oppression is what we do in the West. What they do in the Middle East is 'their culture'.[2]

It's My Culture So I'll Do What I Want To

The 'it's my culture' excuse is frequently wheeled out by groups who wish to continue practices that would otherwise be regarded as unacceptable, or at least challenged. In particular, the need for 'religious toleration' or 'cultural toleration' is routinely used to justify special treatment.

Unlike the rest of the population, Sikhs in Britain have since 1976 been exempted from the requirement to wear crash helmets on motorcycles. Sikhs have also been exempted from the general prohibition on carrying knives in public. Muslims are permitted to produce *halal* meat by stringing up animals by their heels and cutting their throats, without stunning. The government permits this practice 'out of respect for the religious freedoms and fundamental beliefs of people of this country'.[1] Hard Multiculturalism has legitimised this. Soft Multiculturalism, on the other hand, would suggest that anybody should be permitted to be a member of any religion, but not be rendered exempt from the law of the land on account of their faith.

In May 2004 the Commission for Racial Equality published a document in which it outlined guidelines for businesses on ways in which they should provide prayer rooms and give religious holidays to non-Christians. Business leaders claim the cost of implementing the proposals could be £100 million a year.[2] The right of Muslim women to wear *hijabs* in schools has exercised the minds of many in Britain where it otherwise contravenes rules on school uniform, and, more acutely, many in France, where *burkhas* are often seen as an affront to the country's secularist ethos. In June 2004, a 15-year-old Muslim schoolgirl from Luton lost a lengthy battle for the right to wear to class a *jilbab*—the full-length gown worn by many Muslim women that covers all of the body except the face and the hands. The Muslim Council of Britain said it was 'very surprised and concerned' by the judgment.[3] If the school had no uniform, then it would have been an unfair decision, but if it flouted uniform rules, then the ruling should be viewed as perfectly legitimate. Special treatment should not be afforded so as merely to avoid offending cultural sensibilities— something that many of the girl's co-religionists appreciate. 'For her to insist on such a trivial matter and miss two years of her schooling shows where her priorities lay,' wrote Dr Ghayasuddin Siddiqui of the Muslim Parliament to the *Independent*: 'Human rights and multiculturalism should not be used as a licence for unreasonableness.' Parvez Manzoor of Elstree concurred: '[W]e should teach our children to respect the law (as the Quran enjoins upon all Muslims) and not adopt a confrontational and arrogant attitude against all teachings of Islam.'[4] In March this year, however, the High Court overturned the decision, saying that the girl in question, Shabina Begum, had been denied the 'right to education and to manifest her religious beliefs'.[5]

Fashioning law around faith and culture has set both worrying and bizarre precedents. In January 2001, a Rastafarian who offered marijuana to an undercover policeman was spared a prison sentence when a judge said his consumption of the drug was 'very much bound up' with his beliefs. Having explained to the judge that his religious and cultural beliefs permitted him to smoke and sell cannabis, Rasta Brown, 37, was given a diminished sentence of 150 hours' community service.[6] To be consistent, drink-driving laws should not apply to any priest found in charge of a vehicle having downed a bottle of claret who believes it represents (or contains the real presence of) the blood of Christ.

In April 1997 a man who believed himself to be the twentieth-century reincarnation of King Arthur had his sword and ritual dagger confiscated in a demonstration in Trafalgar Square, London. But later that November, Arthur Uther Pendragon—or, to give him his official ceremonial title, Honoured Pendragon of the Glastonbury Order of Druids, Official Swordbearer of the Secular Order of Druids and Titular Head of the Loyal Arthurian Warbands—had his weapons returned to him by a judge at Southwark crown court. After consulting a professor of history at Bristol University, Judge Stephen Robbins was satisfied that Pendragon was a 'genuine druid' who needed his 3ft-long sword for ceremonial purposes.[7] Let us be thankful that Britain does not have an Aztec community.

In 1998, the International Fund for Animal Welfare undertook a campaign against the continued, but now prohibited, practice of Canadian sealers skinning seals alive and removing their penises to be sold as aphrodisiacs. 'My family has gone sealing for generations', protested one Newfoundlander. 'It's a vital part of our culture.'[8] The Chukchi people of Russia's far north have also been exempted from the international whaling ban as, in the words of the Guardian, it has been 'deemed a traditional part of their culture'.[9] Whatever one thinks about the banning of such customs, the argument should focus on the capacity of animals to feel pain, and the dietary needs of those who hunt animals, rather than any (often spurious) claims about cultural heritage.

As we saw in the case of the anthropologist and the small-pox vaccine, the elevation of culture over human health and well-being can be witnessed in regard to the subject of deafness. Many with partial or total hearing impairment regard themselves as part of a 'deaf culture', and consider treatment to alleviate their condition 'a sell-out'. A group called 'Deaf Pride' was formed at Gallaudet University in Washington DC in 1988, and soon successfully blocked the appointment of a hearing university president.[10] Since then, scientists, working on a cure for deafness, through developments in cochlear implant surgery, stem cell therapy and gene therapy, have been met with hostility from members of the 'deaf community'. According to the *New Scientist* reporter, Pat Hagan, many people who are profoundly deaf from an early age define themselves as 'a minority with their own rich culture and language'. They thus 'believe they are not sick and do not need curing' and have 'a personal right to remain deaf', and have even ostracised those that have sought treatment to improve their hearing.[11]

The journalist Fiona Leney faced a similar experience. She had planned to have her son given a cochlear implant, which can allow even someone who is profoundly deaf to acquire useful hearing, and went to a parents support group to talk about the issue. Another mother, who had a deaf child, informed Leney: 'what you're proposing doing to your child is the equivalent of rape'. The woman's husband concurred: 'After all, you have to accept that our deaf children don't really belong to us, they're members of the deaf community.'[12] In 2002 a deaf lesbian couple in America deliberately sought artificial insemination from a friend with five generations of deafness in his family so that their child could be born deaf. They protested they wanted the child to have the same impairment. The baby was consequently born profoundly deaf in his left ear and partly deaf in his right. Candy McCullough, partner to Sharon Duchesneau, defended her decision on cultural grounds: 'Why shouldn't parents be able to go ahead and pick a [deaf] donor if that's what they want? They should have that option. They can feel related to that culture, bonded with that culture.'[13]

Even those most unlikely apologists for multi-culturalism, the Far Right, now resorts to the culture excuse. The British National Party has ceased using the language of race, and ostensibly aspires to preserve 'British culture'. 'We embrace and cherish the native cultural diversity within the British Isles',[14] it says—no bad thing in itself, if anyone believed that this was anything but a euphemism for its racist agenda. In America, in the long-running battle to have the Confederate battle flag removed from the state flag of South Carolina, the semantics have also changed, with those seeking to uphold the status quo asserting that the Dixie Flag is 'a symbol of heritage'.[15]

A more gruesome example of the culture excuse is in the realm of 'honour killings' in Britain, of which an estimated 20 have occurred since 1995. According to Commander Andrew Baker, Head of Scotland Yard's Serious Crime Directorate, there were 12 honour killings in Britain in 2003. At the end of 2004, British police forces were investigating 117 murders as 'honour killings'.[16] These are just the extreme examples: the Southall Black Sisters, a help group for women from ethnic minorities, receives 2,000 inquiries every year from women concerned with domestic violence.[17] Who knows how many acts go unreported? But the fact that the suicide rate among British Asian women is four times the national average does not bode well.[18]

The victim in these 'honour killings' is normally a wife suspected of having been unfaithful to her husband, or a daughter suspected of having had pre-marital sexual intercourse. In such cases, the woman is deemed to have brought shame to her family. In Middle Eastern and South Asian culture, a great emphasis is place on the concepts of shame and honour, and it is women who are charged with upholding a family's honour. Any transgression on her behalf can have grave consequences. Contrary to popular assumption, 'honour killings' have little to do with Islam, and more to do with the continuation of Asian tribal customs that pre-date the coming of Islam. For instance, honour killings have been carried out by Hindu, Sikh and Christian Asians.

The manner of the killings in Britain has often been very brutal. In June 1995, Tasleem Begum, 20, was killed by her brother-in-law, Shabir Hussain. He ran her over in his car, reversed over her body and sped forward once more, crushing her three times. In October 2002, 16-year-old Heshu Yones, from West London, was stabbed 11 times by her 48-year-old father, Abdulla, who then slit her throat—a Kurd, he had disapproved of Heshu's British Arab boyfriend. That year, Yasmin Akhtar, 35, was kidnapped, strangled to death and then set on fire after she filed for a divorce from her husband, Mohammed Jamil. Also in 2002, in Manor Park, East London, Anita Gindha who was 22 and pregnant, was garrotted at home as her toddler son looked on. A Sikh, she had fled Pakistan from an arranged marriage. In September 2003, Birmingham man Rafaqat Hussain admitted murdering his 21-year-old cousin Sahjda Bibi. She was stabbed to death as she dressed for her wedding to an older divorcee of whom her family is said to have disapproved.[19] In Marseilles, Ghofrane Haddaoui, 23, a Tunisian born-French woman, was recently stoned to death for refusing the advances of a teenage boy.[20]

Had these vicious murders in Britain been inter-racial—as in the case of Stephen Lawrence—we would have heard a lot more about them; had they been inter-racial, we certainly would have had an enquiry along the lines of the Macpherson report. Yet the comparative silence, from those who fear to interfere, is troubling. Is 'culture' being used as an excuse for murder? Dr Nazand Begikhani of Kurdish Women's Action Against Honour Killings suspects so. She listened with horror at the Old Bailey in the case over the murder of Heshu, when Judge Neil Denison said that he would take cultural customs into consideration in the sentencing of her killer. 'If her father gets a lesser sentence as a result of cultural factors, it diminishes Heshu's life' she told the *Daily Express* in October 2003. Likewise, the killer of Tasleem Begum claimed that the balance of his mind had been altered by the great shame she had brought to the family. The plea was accepted and the judge sentenced him to three years imprisonment for manslaughter, not murder.[21] Marai Larasi, who works to protect the victims of honour

8

The Price of Multiculturalism

State-sanctioned multiculturalism has not brought about improved inter-cultural and inter-racial relations. It may be argued that the opposite has occurred; we are now far more divided. Consider one case study. The veteran anti-fascist campaigner and broadcaster Kenan Malik has observed with growing despair the results of multiculturalist policies in the city of Bradford, West Yorkshire. Malik's 2001 online essay 'The Trouble With Multiculturalism' is a compelling and depressing account of how state-sponsored multiculturalism in this city has resulted in its different ethnic groups now living isolated, parallel lives, in a climate of mutual suspicion and antagonism.[1]

As Malik retells, the shift from campaigning for racial equality to cultural equality had its genesis in the city in April 1976, when 24 people were arrested in a riot in the city's Mannigham area between Asian youth and National Front demonstrators. This riot led to the formation of the Asian Youth Movement, which sought to protect Asians against white racists. In 1981, 12 Asian youths faced conspiracy charges for making petrol bombs to use against racists. They argued that they were acting in self-defence, and won their cases. Consequently, Bradford council, wary of the Asian community's growing militancy, drew up equal opportunity statements, established race relations units, and began a programme of funding Asian organisations. In a 12-point statement, it declared the city to be a 'multiracial city' and asserted that every section of its community had 'an equal right to maintain its own identity, culture, language, religion and customs.'

In an attempt to placate the militant religious leaders, the council then helped to establish and fund the Bradford Council of Mosques in 1981. So as to deflect accusations of favouritism, it consequently set up in 1984 the Federation of Sikh Organisations and the Vishwa Hindu Parishad. 'The consequence was to create division and tensions within and between different Asian communities, as each fought for a greater allocation of council funding', states Malik. While Bradford had, since the Second World War, been largely segregated along racial lines, in the mid-1980s the Asian community began to fragment along religious lines. Muslims, Sikhs and Hindus began to live in separate areas, going to separate schools, working in separate business. The council accentuated this trend by establishing community organisations and youth centres to cater for different ethnic and religious affiliations. Now bedevilled with inter-ethnic tension, the Asian Youth Movement, the organisation created to help Asians help themselves, was disbanded.

Inter-racial and intra-ethnic minority antagonism has been charted elsewhere. In the opinion of the commentator Darcus Howe, racial tensions between ethnic minorities are at their worst level for 50 years. His 2004 four-part television documentary, *Who You Callin' a Nigger?* made for grim viewing, documenting the hatred and acts of violence between West Indians and Somalians in south London, and West Indians and Pakistanis in the West Midlands. Howe also fell foul of those who want to strangle all debate. The black British newspaper, *New Nation*, took exception to this as well as to Howe's other programmes, one exploring sexual relations between African slaves and their masters, another revealing financial corruption in Christian organisations in Nigeria. *New Nation* printed the email address and telephone number of the executive producer of Channel 4, Narinder Minhas, who was subsequently subjected to threatening telephone calls and physical threats.[2]

Malik recalls that from the 1960s to the early 1980s the three main issues for anti-racists were draconian immigration controls, the fight against racist attacks and police brutality. In contrast, he observed, '[b]y the mid-1980s the political struggles that had dominated the fight against racism in the 1960s and '70s had become transformed into battles over cultural issues. Political struggles unite across ethnic or cultural divisions; cultural struggles inevitably fragment. Since state funding was now linked to cultural identity, so different groups began asserting their particular identities more fiercely. The shift from the political to the cultural arena helped entrench old divisions and to create new ones.'[3]

The programme of assigning funds on the basis of ethnic background has had all too predictable results. State-sponsored multiculturalism has led to cities such as Bradford, Burnley, and Oldham fissuring along sectarian lines, and to heightening racist tensions between whites and Asians—with white people feeling 'the other lot' are getting favourable treatment from their local council. In April 2003 a Commons report by the Housing Planning and Local Government and the Regions Committee concluded that the deployment of Government funds to areas in the North of England had only heightened racial strife. 'Focusing resources on predominantly white council estates or Asian area of run-down private housing could cause serious resentment in the area that did not receive funding', and the programme could have contributed to the disturbances witnessed in Bradford, Burnley and Oldham in 2001.[4] The rise of the BNP in the north, where some of its members sit as councillors, is the result of white people seeing themselves discriminated against by local authorities.

According to a *Times Educational Supplement* study of 2003, schools in these three northern towns had by that time become the most racially segregated in the country. One in four primary schools in Bradford had become more than 70 per cent Asian, while half had become totally white. Meanwhile, the failure to promote integration has had its predictable effect: disintegration. According to a Mori poll of May 2002, most Britons believed that race relations had deteriorated in the previous ten years. A third of white people said they did not mix with ethnic minorities at work, and nearly two-thirds did not meet socially. Four out of ten ethnic minority respondents said that they had suffered racial prejudice, as did one in ten of white people polled. The corollary of this policy of divide and rule is the alienation of the British Islamic populace, of which, according to a *Guardian* survey of November 2004, 61 per cent want British courts to incorporate *sharia* principles in courts, 58 per cent believe that anyone who insults Islam should face criminal prosecution, and 88 per cent want schools and workplaces to accommodate Muslim prayer times as part of their normal working day.[5] State-sponsored multiculturalism has set different British communities against each other.

Yet this apartheid by stealth is not a process that the majority of the British populace desires. A September 2004 poll for YouGov showed that both white and non-white Britons did actually prefer integration, with 70 per cent of whites believing ethnic minorities were too isolated, and 65 per cent of respondents from ethnic minorities agreeing.[6] The same poll related the statistic that 92 per cent of both categories believed that no one should be given special treatment merely on account of their ethnicity.

Bradford's fate had been foreseen a long time beforehand by one figure. The dire results of forced education according to perceived cultural sensibilities, or the idea, as one teacher put it, that 'all children [should] have someone from their own culture teaching them',[7] were prophesied 20 years ago. In 1985, Ray Honeyford, the headteacher of Drummond Middle School in Bradford, warned that the programme of promoting multiculturalism in schools was going to have a malign effect.

He said that the fear of offending Pakistani and
Bangladeshi communities was leading to the ghettoisation of education establishments, and that English was
being relegated to a secondary language. As he later
recalled: 'my philosophy at that time [was] a belief in
integration, and a rejection of both racial prejudice and
multiculturalism, which I felt from experience was
dangerously divisive and contained the seeds of future
conflict.'[8]

For making the rather innocuous and sensible point
that English should be taught as a first language in
schools, and that promoting Asian languages would lead
to 'white flight', Honeyford was vilified by liberal-left
commentators and local politicians, condemned as a
racist, suspended, and, at the age of 51, forced into early
retirement—even though Bradford Council's wish to
pursue a multicultural educational agenda had not been
asked for by the local Asian population, and was
sometimes against the wishes of British Asian parents
themselves.[9] Two years later, in 1986, a Bristol teacher
who had lent his vocal support to Honeyford was asked
not to return to his school, after his colleagues told him
that they 'no longer wished to work with him'.[10] Today,
Drummond school has been renamed as Iqra School, and
is almost 100 per cent ethnically Asian.

Still, however, the Government pursues its agenda of
promoting a multiethnic agenda in schools. The *Education
for All* report, published in 1985, purported to investigate
the 'educational needs and attainments of pupils of West
Indian origin'. Lord Swann, who headed the report, and
his team, called for the implementation of a multiculturalist curriculum as an important means of
addressing racism in schools. Since then many education-
alists have implemented its recommendations, even
among schools that did not have a diverse ethnic make-
up.

But whereas multiculturalism used only to be erron-
eously used as a synonym for multiracialism, it is now

often used as a byword for multireligiosity. The first state-funded Sikh school was opened in December 1999, and in June 2004 a policy document published by Muslims on Education recommended the founding of more Muslim state schools, the separation of sexes, and more compulsory religious education. As the novelist Tim Lott pointed out: 'we hope that any new schools will teach the fact that more than 4,000 homosexuals have been executed in Iran since the Islamic revolution of 1979, and that in the United Arab Emirates husbands have the right to assault their wives, and that in Saudi Arabia women cannot vote, drive or show their faces in public'.[11]

It is admirable, at a scholarly level, that a child may be taught Urdu or Arabic, but it will not equip that youngster for life in the adult world in Britain. Permitting gypsies to be excused from mainstream education on account of their nomadic culture, and excusing Muslim girls from biology lessons, deprive the needy of a vital education. A poor grasp of English will serve as a handicap in the workplace, thus increasing 'social exclusion' levels among Asian minorities. In promoting other languages in place of English, the state is depriving millions of the chance to better themselves in the employment market. This generates a vicious circle. Upon seeing members of ethnic minorities in poverty, the state throws money at them. This often entails promoting minority languages or cultural awareness. The person at whom this cash is aimed thus remains in poverty. The government reacts with yet further funds. And so on. Multiculturalism is not merely an impoverished ideal, it keeps those it aspires to help in a state of poverty. This is the poverty of multiculturalism.

The lamentable results of ethnically-sensitive pedagogy have been witnessed elsewhere, specifically in Australia and the United States. *In Losing Our Language: How Multicultural Classroom Instruction Is Undermining Our Children's Ability to Read, Write, and Reason*, for instance, Sandra Stotsky undertook a study of how multiculturally-sensitive English textbooks introduced in the US since the 1960s have been far less rigorous and demanding than those that they replaced. Rather than pursuing competence and excellence in the English language, the curriculum, composed by those alarmed at the low academic performance among many black and Hispanic Americans, has urged pupils to raise their 'self-image' and recognise 'the positive contributions of minority groups in this country'. It has merely led to a decline in literacy and academic performance among black Americans.[12]

In Australia, the shift from teaching Aboriginals in integrated mainstream education towards having them taught separately has had similar unfortunate effects. The curriculum there is bilingual, and subjects are concerned with teaching Aboriginal traditions and with cultivating a sense of ethnic awareness and ethnic pride among pupils. As Roger Sandall noted, in a 1999 Sydney seminar the principal of a Darwin college told how, between 1965 and 1975, Aboriginal students from the outlying bush communities arrived with sixth-grade literacy levels. By 1990, these had fallen to third-grade level. 'Today they arrive at his college completely illiterate.'[13]

Discouraging people from speaking English not only handicaps them for the workplace, it is also profligate. Consider the cost of having bilingual street signs in London's Southall and Brick Lane districts to cater for the Asian community, which concurrently help to depress levels of English literacy. Local government throughout Britain is always keen to provide multilingual services. In July 2004, for instance, residents of West London received a leaflet concerning the proposed tram development. It was also available in Arabic, Bengali, Chinese, Greek, Gujarati, Hindi, Punjabi, Turkish, Urdu and Vietnamese. In October 2004, my local council, Hammersmith & Fulham in London, asked residents to 'have their say' in a survey on how to tackle crime: 'If you would like any part of this document interpreted, please phone...' a number giving residents the opportunity to hear the survey in Russian, Polish, French, Spanish, Albanian, Amharic, Portuguese, Somali, Punjabi, Gujarati, Hindi, Urdu, Farsi or Arabic. Naturally, the same survey also posed the question 'What is your ethnic group?' (Answers, 'White', 'Mixed Race', 'Asian or Asian British', 'Black or Black British', 'Chinese' or 'other ethnic group').[14]

London's 999 emergency services recently decided to employ linguists to translate emergency calls into 150 languages, from Afrikaans to Zulu. This is owing to the fact that three million out of London's eight million inhabitants do not speak English as a first language. Speaking to the London *Evening Standard* in July 2004, Professor Tim Connell, the Director of Language Studies at City University, welcomed the move: 'It is really key that public services embrace these languages because everyone has a right to basic services.'[15] But translators do not come for free. If everyone did speak English as a first language, such money could be invested in the emergency services and save more lives. Saving lives should take precedence over promoting cultural diversity.

Many recognise that an ethnically sensitive curriculum is actively detrimental to ethnic minorities. A survey of 2002 reported that 75 per cent of blacks and 68 per cent of Asians supported the idea that British history and culture should be taught in classes, and that acquiring a good standard of English was essential.[16] The fact is that many Britons, of all hues, simply don't like or want enforced multiculturalism, as was illustrated in British Airways' disastrous (and now reversed) decision to take the Union Flag off its tail-fins in 1996 and to replace it with exotic 'ethnic patterns'. So too is the increasing propensity of Asians and blacks to follow England football team, and the fact that they no longer feel afraid to fly the St George Cross during sporting tournaments.

We seek to undermine a traditional understanding of British culture in other avenues. The deliberate neglect of British history in schools for decades now means that

British adults today know very little about their own history. A survey for Channel 4 in October 2004 showed that 60 per cent did not know who defeated Harold II at the Battle of Hastings; 70 per cent didn't know who was the first king to sit both on the thrones of Scotland and England; 71 per cent did not know which king signed the Magna Carta.[17] Yet the recent success of history television series by David Starkey, Simon Schama and Richard Holmes—old-fashioned 'history from above' programmes that are delivered in a traditional, monologue, lecturer style not seen since A.J.P. Taylor—illustrates that people do actually want to know about Britain's past. The surprise success of George Courtauld's *Pocket Book of Patriotism*, a 64-page history of Britain for the ignorant yet curious, mirrors this trend. The appetite for and popularity of these television shows and books is a sad indictment of the way history has been taught in schools.

Still, where the people seek to assimilate, the Government maintains its effort to divide. The census is now printed in several languages, and, in 2001, for the first time, the population of England and Wales were invited to register their religion. Categories included Hindu, Sikh, and Jewish, which are effectively quasi-ethnic classifications. It was not mandatory to tick this part of the census, but it was obligatory to register your ethnic category. In so many spheres, local and central government are encouraging British people to regard themselves not as British first and black, Asian, Scottish, etc. as second, but as some separate ethnicity first, and British last—if at all.

9

The Challenge to The Left

Critics of Hard Multiculturalism are often perceived to be politically conservative, and this perception is mostly legitimate. In recent years, however, there has emerged within the Left the growing realisation that this orthodoxy has not been as successful as its advocates of the 1960s and 1970s had hoped. Those who believe in bigger government and higher taxes have begun to appreciate that Hard Multiculturalism is actually antithetical to their political aspirations—and for reasons that are, in retrospect, rather obvious.

It was not always the way. From Edmund Burke to Roger Scruton, traditional English conservatives (or what are sometimes called 'palaeoconservatives', as opposed to neoconservatives, who have no disagreement with the Enlightenment) have attached greater importance to place, tradition and culture, while those on the Left had a far greater affinity with the tenets of the Enlightenment and the idea of the brotherhood of humanity. As opposed to conservatives, 'progressives' are inclined to believe in the organic nature of a society, that we are all part of a greater thing, and that we all have our part to play in helping to bring about solidarity and equality. This is why theorists of the welfare state were often nationalists. In his 1931 book *Equality*, R. H. Tawney wrote that 'what a community requires ... is a common culture, because, without it, it is not a community at all'. Similarly, in his report of 1942, William Beveridge recognised that a system of social insurance would require 'a sense of national unity overriding the interests of any class or section'.[1] It was entirely logical for the British nation to vote out Winston Churchill in 1945. It was because the country was then experiencing a surge of solidarity, and a belief that the nation was 'all in it together', that it could vote in a Labour Government in such vast numbers. Left-liberals are today given to deriding patriotism, but socialism requires patriotism.

Hard Multiculturalism in subsequent years has acted only to divide the population into groupsicles of competing ethnicities who feel they have nothing in common with each other. What is more, redistributive politics are not accepted when people feel they have to share with strangers, with people who are 'not like us'. Alan Wolfe and Jyttee Klausen reminded us so in an article in the liberal monthly *Prospect* in December 2000. 'Solidarity and diversity are both desirable objectives. Unfortunately, they can also conflict. A sense of solidarity creates a readiness to share with strangers, which in turn underpins a thriving welfare state. But it is easier to feel solidarity with those who broadly share your values and way of life. Modern progressives committed to diversity often fail to acknowledge this.' Diversity and solidarity, sound-bites of the Left, can be mutually antagonistic.

The argument was elaborated by *Prospect*'s editor David Goodhart at the beginning of 2004. He cited findings by evolutionary and social psychologists that there is an innate tendency among humans to favour our own group, and that we always perceive people to belong to the 'out-group' or the 'in-group'. We are prepared to share only with those whom we regard as belonging to the latter. This is why redistributive policies work in fairly homogenous countries such as Sweden, a place in which multiculturalism is not encouraged. This is also why in a country such as the United States, which is sub-divided into numerous sub-ethnic groups, a welfare state has failed to blossom. People only feel comfortable in sharing with those they regard as 'one of us'. [2]

Reaction to David Goodhart's essay, reprinted in the *Guardian*, was mixed, varying from those who tentatively agreed, to those taking offence, and to Hard Multiculturalists playing the 'racist' card. In a letter to the newspaper, Ben Carrington of Eastbourne, East Sussex, wrote: 'David Goodhart's disingenuous argument takes us back 40 years in its deliberate conflation of "immigrants" and "ethnic minorities" into an alien "other", supposedly at odds with the (never defined) "common culture" of the presumably white majority ... Presumably ... Goodhart would agree with other right-wing commentators in suggesting the England teams should similarly avoid having too many brown and black faces in their ranks to prevent cultural fragmentation.' 'Thatcher put it more honestly and succinctly', wrote A. Sivanandan of the Institute of Race Relations, accusing Goodhart of 'xeno-racism'.[3]

The ill-tempered reaction by Trevor Phillips, the head of the Commission for Racial Equality, illustrated how we have failed to move on from the days of the Ray Honeyford affair: 'Is this the wit and wisdom of Enoch Powell? Jottings from the BNP leader's weblog? ... The xenophobes should come clean. Their argument is not about immigration at all. They are liberal Powellites.'[4] The right-wing commentator Peter Hitchens made the obvious point which opponents of racism have seldom recognised:

> To insist on cultural integration is the exact opposite of racialism, and the ludicrous smearing of cultural conservatives as 'racists' by so many on the left is not just wicked but also witless, ignorant gibberish... The left's implacable hostility to racialism is the best thing about it, and its cultural victory over prejudice and bigotry one of its greatest achievements.'[5]

It is peculiar that many who are the inheritors of the secular, rational Enlightenment tradition, and who call themselves 'progressives', have not only come to be apologists for ethnic separateness, but—under the ostensible banner of respecting diversity—have come to defend organised religion and irrationalism. When Shabina Begum lost her high court battle to wear strict Islamic dress to school in June 2004, some left-leaning commentators decried this as racist and oppressive. The following month, the Mayor of London, Ken Livingstone, vowed that the British would never follow the French example and ban headscarves in schools. 'The French ban is the most reactionary proposal to be considered by any parliament in Europe since the Second World War', he said (with not a little exaggeration). 'I am determined London's Muslims should never face similar restrictions. It marks a move towards religious intolerance which we in Europe swore never to repeat, having witnessed the devastating effects of the Holocaust.'[6]

Whatever happened to the Left's suspicion of organised religion? What of the idea that faiths should be tolerated only in the private sphere, and not funded in the public sphere? It took the Vice-President of the National Secular Society to argue: 'If a line is not drawn, the next demand may be for permission to wear a *burkha*, or to be excluded from lessons taught by men, or to be excused lessons which contradict the Koran. This could be followed by the desire to be absent from lessons five times a day.'[7]

As Stephen Eric Bronner laments in *Reclaiming the Enlightenment*, this is part of a wider malaise, the symptom of a deeper corruption of the Left.[8] Under the spell of relativist postmodernist theory and despairing of the failure of the Socialist experiments of the twentieth century, erstwhile progressives have sought intellectual refuge in 'identity politics' and the veneration of 'culture'. They have come to resemble the conservatives of old. Todd Gitlin notes this strange reverse in *The Twilight of Common Dreams: Why America is Wracked by Culture Wars*:

> Between Left and Right there has taken place a curious reversal. Throughout the nineteenth and twentieth centuries, the Left believed in a common human condition, the Right in fundamental differences among classes, nations, races. The Left wanted collective acts of renewal, the Right endorsed primordial ties of tradition and community against all disruptions ... Today it is the Right that speaks a language of commonalities. Its rhetoric of global markets and global freedoms has something of the old universalist ring. To be on the Left, meanwhile, is to doubt that one can speak of humanity at all.[9]

Edmund Burke, Benjamin Disraeli and Michael Oakshott are palaeoconservative heroes, and detractors of the Enlightenment. Since Hayek and Popper, however, many on the Right have come to embrace the universalist aspects of the Enlightenment. Simultaneously, many on the Left have moved in the other direction.

In academe, there are relatively few voices of the Left still championing Reason, such as Noam Chomsky; Brian Barry, author of *Culture and Equality* (2001); Stephen Eric Bronner; Richard Wolin, author of *The Seduction of Unreason* (2004); and the late Susan Moller Okin, whose *Is Multiculturalism Bad For Women?* (1999) gave the answer 'yes' to its title. When she concluded that gender equality was impossible to achieve among societies that practice polygamy, forced marriage or female genital mutilation, she faced the accusation of being dogmatically attached to western liberalism.

In British society, one can count a few public figures on the Left who are fearless enough to stand up against unreason that is smuggled under the banner of culture: one thinks of Richard Dawkins; the journalists Mick Hume, Francis Wheen and Polly Toynbee, the last of whom laments that '[t]he natural allies of the rationalists have decamped. The left embraces Islam for its anti-Americanism. Liberals and progressives have had a collective softening of the brain and weakening of the knees'[10] (although Toynbee's quarrel, as with Ludovic Kennedy's, is less with multiculturalism than with organised religion). Another to put his head above the parapet is the gay rights campaigner Peter Tatchell, who rebutted accusations that his effort to ban homophobic reggae singers is racist. 'Some defend violently anti-gay reggae music on the grounds that homophobia is "part of Jamaican culture". Racism was part of Afrikaaner culture in apartheid South Africa, but that did not make it right,' Tatchell wrote in the *Guardian* in August 2004:

The real racism is not our campaign against murder music, but most people's indifference to the persecution of gay Jamaicans. No one would tolerate such abuses against white people in Britain; it is racist to allow them to happen to black people in another country.[11]

Peter Wilby, former editor of the left-leaning weekly *New Statesman*, concurs that the multiculturalist agenda often detracts from the real needs of the poor. With unemployment in Britain among men of Pakistani, Bangladeshi and blacks of Caribbean origin running 10 to 15 per cent higher than it is among white men:

[w]hat concerns most ethnic-minority people is not whether their daughters can wear the *hijab* at school, or the council sponsors *Diwali* celebrations, or lessons include references to Arab scientists. They want jobs and good wages.[12]

The sociologist and philosopher Zygmunt Bauman, a tenacious socialist, agrees:

If insecurity and the paralysing feeling of powerlessness are the two major spectres haunting the poor, 'multiculturalism' and 'moral relativism' must be two of the least topical worries of poorer people.[13]

It has come to a bizarre predicament when, in July 2004, Ken Livingstone saw no objection to welcoming to City Hall an Islamic extremist Muslim cleric who asserted that women who are raped are partly to blame; that husbands should be permitted to hit their wives; and that homosexuality should be punished by 'burning' or 'stoning' to death.[14]

There is an associated malaise among those who resist the imperative to draw attention to the shortcomings of much black British 'gangsta culture', and its glorification of guns and misogyny. When Sacha Baron-Cohen did so through his satirical character 'Ali G', some accused him of racism. But he was merely pointing out that gangsta culture, which is venerated by many white commentators as 'authentic' or the 'voice of the oppressed', will not do. Only when black commentators, such as the football and political commentator Garth Crooks, express their objection to this 'gangsta' culture, does the white liberal intelligentsia take notice. In September 2004, he berated this gangsta street culture as a 'deadly virus' that was destroying the hopes of Britain's young black population. 'As for the youngsters in our community who think they are gangsters: grow up. You are not gangsters or clever. You are kids and it's time to impose zero tolerance', he said. 'Street culture will become a deadly virus ripping indiscriminately through our next generation, robbing millions of their potential.'[15] Similarly, in July 2004, Bill Cosby lent his support to a campaign to stop having West Indian slang taught in London schools, on the grounds that it did a disservice to black children.[16] Anyone who decries the notion that respectability, decency and hard-work are 'white values' does a grave disservice to black children and reinforces age-old racist stereotypes about the uncivilised disposition of black people.

The celebration of ethnic particularism is a betrayal of the socialist ideal that the best way to create a more equal society is to perceive oneself, above anything else, along class lines. Indeed, the culture cult renders impotent any socialist agenda. Celebrating diversity is an unwitting way of implementing a policy of divide and rule. In the words of the left-wing sociologist Brian Barry:

> There is no better way of heading off the nightmare of political action by the economically disadvantaged that might issue in common demands than to set different groups of the disadvantaged against one another.[17]

Too many on the Left have been corrupted by the culture cult and consequently, rather than aspiring towards colour-blindness, they have become obsessed with race and culture. They often pigeonhole and stereotype ethnic minorities, and expect them to have typically 'ethnic' concerns. Television advertisements on the BBC for special programmes dealing with 'black issues' routinely feature inner-city ghettos, rap music and gangs. In March 2004, the black presenter Henry Bonsu lost his job on his BBC London talkshow for being too 'intellectual' and not addressing 'real' black issues such as football and rap music.[18] The state's ethnic radio station, BBC Asian Network, has the predictable clichéd combination of bangra music and debates about racism and Ramadan. In supporting St Patrick's Day festivals, local councils duly expect the 'Irish community' (of which I am, in the state's eyes, officially a member) to put on a green wig and get roaringly drunk.

It is an attitude accurately satirised by John Fardell's comic strip 'The Critics' in *Viz* comic. Natasha and Crispin are an insufferable, politically-correct couple who champion everything non-Western. In one adventure, looking to find an example of genuinely ethnic art, they go to interview the 'up-and-coming playwright, Aisha Peerzada'.

> CRISPIN: So tell, us, Aisha, what's the theme of your first play for The Royal Court?
>
> NATASHA: Forced marriages? Islamic Fundamentalism? Racist firebombings of Asian corner shops?
>
> AISHA: No. That'd be really *boring*. I've written a light musical comedy set on a luxury cruise liner.
>
> [The Critics storm out of her house in disgust]
>
> NATASHA: How one laments the way in which these children of immigrants feel forced to deny their cultural roots...'[19]

10

The End of Multiculturalism?

The debate over culture is controversial, and for many remains a taboo subject. Those who harbour suspicions of the multicultural orthodoxies simply do not speak about it, for fear of being labelled judgmental or racist. For the same reason, others surrender by parroting its mantras. There are signs, however, that people feel more confident in speaking up against the shortcomings of non-Western cultures, and the positive facets of Western civilisation.

This is not to excuse the crimes of the West. Despite the myriad benefits it brought to the world, and its occasional and ostensibly benign but patronising rhetoric of 'taking up the white man's burden', European colonialism was driven by greed and brought oppression to many peoples throughout the globe. Many assume that religious extremism is a characteristic solely of Islam. The massacre of some 30,000 Jews and Muslims in 1099 by Christian Crusader extremists illustrates that it is not. Today, many Christian fundamentalists in the United States would like to see homosexuality punished, and some regard abortion as such a serious crime that they have resorted to murder: seven doctors who carry out abortions have been murdered in the US since 1993.[1]

The British Empire's record in India was certainly patchy, if one takes into account, for instance, the Amritsar Massacre of 1919 or the brutal put-down of the Sepoy Rebellion of 1857-58. In Ireland, British conduct veered from benign to cynical to callous. In the domestic arena, until the nineteenth century, Roman Catholics and Dissenters were not treated as equals in the eyes of the law. Since then, however, the United Kingdom can be proud of its tradition of liberalism and tolerance—certainly in comparison with dictatorial and totalitarian régimes that have come and gone. Consider too the treatment of the indigenous Americans, or, up till the last decade, the apartheid régime of Dutch and British settlers in South Africa. The United States' self-appointed role as policeman of the world today is certainly questionable. While we should champion democracy and liberty at home, to enforce it by military means abroad is a different thing.

Indeed, it has been argued that Western interference in the Middle East has helped to retard their societies. The misogyny that is widespread in the Islamic world is, according to one theory, the product of imperialism. The hardening of attitudes towards women in the nineteenth and twentieth centuries, writes Akbar S. Ahmed in *Islam Under Siege*, was a response to European colonialism:

> There was a loss of confidence, which resulted in a loss of tolerance. Muslim men reacted to this loss, not unnaturally, by doing what they thought was necessary for the protection and integrity of their families. They secluded their women from the prying eyes of foreign troops. *Burkhas*, the black, tent-like attire women wear, became common. Women were restricted to the home.[2]

It is also worth keeping in mind that female suffrage was introduced in Islamic Azerbaijan in 1918 and in Turkey in 1934, whereas in France it only arrived in 1944.

One should not belittle the achievements of non-Western cultures, such as the contribution of the Arab world in the fields of science and medicine, or the progress made by Japan in computer technology. China gave us paper, printing and books. We must exchange what is best from each other and seek to address our mutual faults. Judgmentalism is imperative. For instance, white Britain could learn much from its dispro-portionately wealthier British Indian community, and ask itself why if you are called Patel you are seven times more likely to be a multi-millionaire than if your name is Smith.[3] Is it because Indians have a more entrenched work ethic and closer sense of family? Rather than complaining that the state isn't giving them enough financial support, or bemoaning that 'they come over here and taking all OUR dole money', many white Britons could learn by example.

Neither is it to say that cultures are static, hermetically sealed entities. All cultures and societies evolve and appropriate customs, languages, words, cuisine and legal systems from one other. After all, the English language is a hybrid of Anglo-Saxon and Norman French, West Indian patois has been incorporated into the language of Londoners, England's patron saint was Palestinian, its Royal Family is German, chips are a Belgian invention, tea is from India and the UK's favourite dish is now an Anglicised curry: the famous chicken tikka massala. Much of what we consider to be traditional British culture—particularly the trappings of the monarchy—is a fairly recent invention of the nineteenth century, which has also appropriated many foreign facets.[4]

It is wrong to say, however, that all this renders hopeless the task of judging one culture as better than another. Most people would prefer to live in a country in which people are not persecuted because of their religious or political creed, in which there is equality of opportunity, democratic rule, where the state cannot arbitrarily imprison people, where there exists freedom of association, free speech, and in which men and women are judged not by the colour of their skin, or their cultural background, but by their character.

Some contend that these are eurocentric concepts, and in many respects, that is correct: these ideals germinated and were crystallised in Europe in the age of the Enlightenment. To ignore their source in Christianity would be intellectually dishonest, too: after all, progress is a secularised version of providence, the individual is the soul reinvented, equality a throwback to the biblical notion that we are all created the same, fraternity a rehash of the notion that we are all God's people.

But just because Europe secularised these ideas into those of the Enlightenment, it does not mean the rest of the world cannot embrace them too. The logical corollary of the relativist argument is that, because the number '0' was invented in Asia, Westerners should shun it and revert to Roman numerals, and that, because Ptolemy first postulated that the world is spherical, we should re-embrace the good-old fashioned Western European notion that the world is flat. As Joseph Needham's series of volumes *Science and Civilisation in China* reveals, a smallpox vaccine was developed in China in tenth century AD. In the interests of cultural purity, then, we should let people in Europe die of smallpox.

The West 'invented' the Enlightenment, an invention that also enriches the quality of our lives. Just because European civilisation has had its shortcoming, we should not jettison its positive contribution to world civilisation—something that the radical black Marxist C. L. R. James (1901-1989) recognised. 'I denounce European colonialism', he wrote. 'But I respect the learning and profound discoveries of Western civilisation.'[5] In a similar vein, the anti-colonialist African nationalist Frantz Fanon could assert:

> All the elements of a solution to the great problems of humanity have, at different times, existed in European thought. But Europeans have not carried out in practice the mission that fell to them.[6]

This sentiment, this admiration of Western ways, can be heard today in many Islamic countries. As an Islamophile scholar, Peter Watson, has observed:

> In many Muslim countries today most people would like to get to grips with modernity, rather than return to stifling orthodoxy. We in the West should help them.[7]

It is an outlook echoed by the British journalist Yasmin Alibhai-Brown:

> All enlightened Muslims (yes, there are millions of them) feel a terrible pessimism and foreboding that authoritarianism, philis-

tinism and barbarism are now the hallmarks of most Muslim states and too many Muslim immigrant communities—a barbarism which is killing hope, excellence, ambitions, life itself. We need reformation.[8]

And, as Karen Armstrong has argued in *Islam: A Short History*, democracy is not antithetical to the teachings of the Koran—contrary to the assumption of both some detractors and believers of the religion.[9] For instance, Pakistan, Turkey and Iran have (albeit imperfect) democratic constitutions.

We can be judgmental. We should be judgmental. Occasionally, judgments can be made in a crass manner, like Silvio Berlusconi's remarks made in the wake of the September 11, 2001, attacks. The Italian prime minister opined that the Islamic world was inferior to the Western world: 'we must be aware of the superiority of our civilisation that has guaranteed wellbeing, respect for human rights and—in contrast with Islamic countries—respect for religious and political rights.' He went on to say he hoped that 'the West will continue to conquer peoples, like it conquered communism', even if it meant a confrontation with 'another civilisation, the Islamic one, stuck where it was 1,400 years ago'.[10]

Berlusconi's comments about 'conquering' were certainly unwise, as was his timing, but, while many expressed their 'offence' at his 'insensitive' comments, few attempted to refute his arguments. What many took issue with was his breaking the taboo of non-judgmentalism. We have become so indoctrinated with the notion of cultural relativism that such remarks strike us as archaic and almost blasphemous. In Britain, too, there are signs of change. Lord Carey, the ex-Archbishop of Canterbury, felt confident in March 2004 to speak out against the shortcomings of many authoritarian Middle Eastern régimes. 'It is sad to relate no great invention has come for many hundred years from Muslim countries. Sadly, apart from a few courageous examples, very few Muslim leaders condemn clearly and unconditionally the evil of suicide bombers who kill innocent people.' As with the Robert Kilroy-Silk incident (he made similar remarks with far less elegance, mistakenly referring to Iran as an Arab nation), there was predictable outcry over Carey's remarks. 'This is a disastrous statement', said Manzoor Moghal, chairman of the Federation of Muslim Organisations. 'He has fallen prey to the campaign tactics of racists in this country.'[11] That an Anglican cleric could utter such decidedly non-inclusive and judgmental words was representative of a growing willingness to enter into frank and open debate.

Similarly, the Dutch politician Pim Fortuyn was roundly decried as a 'right-wing extremist' because he questioned multicultural orthodoxies. 'If you try to discuss multiculturalism in the UK you're labelled a racist', he told the *Daily Telegraph*, shortly before he was murdered by an animal rights fanatic. 'But here we're still free to talk, and I say multicultural society doesn't work. We're not living closer, we're living apart.'[12] But at least he had the courage to say so. Fortuyn, who was a homosexual and an ex-Marxist, made the legitimate point that radical Islam threatened Holland's liberal consensus, its pride in equal rights for women and emancipation of gays. The murder of the film-maker Theo van Gogh in 2004, who was an opponent of Islam's treatment of women, illustrated that Holland's experiment with multiculturalism has been far from a success. Indeed, Dutch television viewers were shocked to see interviews with young Dutch Muslims in the aftermath, approving the murder of van Gogh. 'If you insult Islam, you have to pay' was their familiar response.[13] Holland is now experiencing a net outflow if migrants for the first time since 1945, with many citing inter-religious and inter-cultural strife as their motivation.[14]

Concerning the policies of multiculturalism at home, even its former champions have began to recognise that too much diversity has resulted in too much divisiveness. Yasmin Alibhai-Brown concedes that multiculturalism 'risks building barriers between the different tribes that make up Britain today, rather than helping to create a new shared sense of Britishness'.[15] Shortly after berating David Goodhart, Trevor Phillips seemed to have had a rethink on the matter. In April 2004 he declared that it was actually time to 'kill off multiculturalism': 'Multiculturalism does not mean anybody can do anything they like in the name of their culture... Multiculturalism suggests separateness. We are in a different world from the Seventies.'[16] Phillips subsequently elaborated in the *Guardian*: 'Our ideal should be one nation of many faces: one culture integrating many faiths and traditions.'[17]

The Home Office followed a month later, launching a drive to develop a sense of British pride. Its consultation paper, with the oxymoronic title *Strength in Diversity* (rightly) did not ask that people should jettison altogether their ethnic background, but urged 'that all citizens feel a sense of pride in being British and a sense of belonging to this country and each other'. New Labour has also begun to appreciate that its communitarian agenda requires a sense of national cohesiveness. As David Blunkett wrote in March this year: 'In England, too often we have been apologetic in our approach to patriotism',[18] a viewpoint with which Gordon Brown agrees:

> You cannot as a country face up to the huge decisions you've got to make in the modern world unless you do have a sense of shared purpose, and idea of what your destiny as a nation is.[19]

V. S. Naipaul, the Nobel prize-winning author, never a slave to liberal-left dogma, is one of the latest to voice concerns at the legacy of multiculturalism. 'It's all absurd, you know. I think if a man picks himself up and comes to another country he must meet it halfway.' Naipaul, who was born in Trinidad to Indian parents, said:

> [A person] can't say, 'I want the country, I want the laws and the protection, but I want to live in my own way'. It's wrong. It's

become some kind of racket, this multiculturalism. Jobs for the boys.[20]

It remains to be seen what the Government could do to promote Britishness. By Britishness I mean the understanding that this nation is underpinned by its imperial, Protestant past (as someone raised from a Catholic Irish background, I am happy to acknowledge this), its combination of four nations, its attachment to liberty and tolerance, its constitutional monarchy, its rich language that has given the world some of the finest authors, its indefatigable island nation status. We should not ignore the role played by the Empire in forging Britishness. Indeed, nothing reminds us so visually of our imperial past than the racial composition of this country, of which many of the inhabitants are the descendents of immigrants from the Commonwealth.

The solution is not, as David Blunkett suggested in December 2002, to require all immigrants to swear an 'oath of allegiance' to Britain. Nor should anyone be compelled to speak English or 'forced' to integrate. No society that calls itself liberal should employ such authoritarian methods. The muscle of the State is not the solution; rather, it is the problem. Central and local government should cease financing schemes that keep ethnic minorities ghettoised and impoverished in the first place, and which simultaneously accentuate inter-racial envy.

It is a shame that only now have so-called progressives have come to appreciate what conservatives have been saying for 40 years: that a country can remain cohesive only if there is at least a residual sense of togetherness, in other words, patriotism. This is not to venerate ethnicity, it is to stress that states can only function if their inhabitants (of whatever colour) feel they have the same values as those of their neighbours. The need to feel part of a group is a human instinct, but the values of the

Enlightenment can temper this instinct and help us to achieve a just and peaceable society.

Respect for individuals is not the same as respect for groups. The former is an imperative for any democracy; the latter must be questioned. Diversity is good, but too much of it can be positively dangerous. A nation that is acutely divided along ethnic and cultural lines will not stand. The Soviet Union and Yugoslavia were both genuinely multicultural societies.[21] The latter was driven to bloody conflict on account of its mixed bag of ethnic groupings, each of which suspected that other groupings were receiving preferable treatment. The Russian Federation's protracted conflict in Chechnya reminds us that its multicultural troubles are far from resolved.

Taken to its logical extreme, non-judgmental toleration means anarchy. If there is no right and wrong, and only 'culture', then anything goes. I can do whatever I like because 'it's my culture'. In the end, might will equal right. Hard Multiculturalism and cultural relativism might lead us down the road to barbarism.

Notes

1: Don't Respect Difference: Ignore Difference

1 *Equality and Diversity: The Way Ahead*, DTI, 2002.

2 Lecture given at the *Institut français*, London, 16 November 2002.

3 Parekh, B., *Rethinking Multiculturalism, Cultural Diversity and Political Theory*, London: Macmillan, 2000, p. 168.

4 See, for example, Gould, S.J., *The Mismeasure of Man*, London: Penguin, 1996.

5 See *Birmingham Post*, 22 November 2004.

6 *Irish Post*, 22 January 2005.

7 *Sun*, 13 November 2004.

8 Parekh, *Rethinking Multiculturalism, Cultural Diversity and Political Theory*, 2000, p. 170.

9 *Prospect*, February 2004.

2: A Brief History of Cultural Relativism

1 Herodotus, *The Histories* (440BC), London: Penguin, 1988, pp. 219-20.

2 Quoted in Levy, N., *Moral Relativism, A Short Introduction*, Oxford: Oneworld, 2002, p. 91.

3 Parekh, B., *Rethinking Multiculturalism, Cultural Diversity and Political Theory*, London: Macmillan, 2000, p. 52.

4 Berlin, I., *Vico and Herder, Two Studies in the History of Ideas*, London: Hogarth Press, 1976, p. 145.

5 Cited in Parekh, *Rethinking Multiculturalism, Cultural Diversity and Political Theory*, 2000, p. 68.

6 Lukacs, J., *At the End of an Age*, London: Yale University Press, 2002, p. 7.

71

7   One interesting manifestation of this in popular culture can be
     witnessed in the science-fiction television programme *Star Trek*
     (1966-69). In it, the crew of the *USS Enterprise* were ordered to obey
     the 'Prime Directive', which dictated they were not to interfere in
     alien civilisations or offer them ways of improving their societies.

8   Foucault, M., *Power, The Essential Works of Foucault 1954-1984*,
     London: Penguin, 1994, p. 8.

9   Cited in *Reason*, June 1999.

10   Quoted in *Prospect*, April 2003.

11   Berndt, C.H. and Berndt, R.M., *The Barbarians*, Middlesex: Penguin,
     1971, p. 20.

12   Berlin, I., *Vico and Herder, Two Studies in the History of Ideas*, London:
     Hogarth Press, 1976, p. 210.

13   Rosaldo, R., *Culture and Truth: The Remaking of Social Analysis*,
     Boston, Massachusetts: Beacon Press, 1993, p. 196.

14   Maalouf, A., *On Identity*, London: The Harvill Press, 2000, p. 107.

3: Civilisation and Its Malcontents

1   Malik, K., 'All cultures are not equal', *spiked-online.com*, 28 May
     2002.

2   Gray, J., ' Beyond Reasonable Doubt', *New Statesman*, 31 May 2004.

3   Bauman, Z., *Modernity and the Holocaust*, Cambridge University
     Press (1989), p. 8.

4   *Guardian*, 25 May 2004; *Evening Standard*, 24 May 2004. This anti-
     human sentiment was prefigured in Billy Wilder's Cold War satire
     film *One, Two, Three* (1961), in which an East German communist,
     furious at a comrade's defection to the decadent West, proclaims
     'Maybe we should liquidate the whole human race and start over
     again!'—to which James Cagney's character replies: 'Any world
     that can produce the Taj Mahal, William Shakespeare and striped
     toothpaste can't be all bad.'

5   Goldberg, D., *Racist Culture*, Oxford: Blackwell, 1993, p. 29.

6   Said, E., *Culture and Imperialism*, London: Chatto & Windus, 1989, p. 8.

7   Moore, M., *Stupid White Men*, London: Penguin, 2002, p. 60.

8   Arthur Hippler, cited in Edgerton, R.B., *Sick Societies*, New York: The Free Press, 1992, p. 37.

9   Cited in Whelan, R., *Wild in Woods, The Myth of the Noble Eco-Savage*, London: IEA, 1999, p. 25.

10 Quoted *Reason*, July 2000; Whelan, *Wild in Woods*, 1999, p. 22; Easterbrook, G., *A Moment on the Earth, The Coming Age of Environmental Optimism*, London: Penguin, 1995, p. 91.

11 Gill, A.A., *Sunday Times*, 28 May 1995.

12 Cited in Leadbeater, C., *Up the Down Escalator: Why the Global Pessimists are Wrong*, London: Viking, 2002, p. 184.

13 Cited in Alibhai-Brown, Y., *Some of My Best Friends Are...*, , London: Politico's, 2004, p. 55.

14 *The Future of Multi-ethnic Britain, The Parekh Report*, London: Profile Books, 2000, 3:30, p. 38.

4: The New Irrationalism

1   'What then is truth? A mobile army of metaphors, metonyms, and anthropomorphisms—in short, a sum of human relations, which have been enhanced, transposed, and embellished poetically and rhetorically, and which after long use seem firm, canonical, and obligatory to a people: truths are illusions about which one has forgotten that is what they are; metaphors which are worn out and without sensuous power; coins which have lost their pictures and now matter only as metal, no longer as coins. We still do not know where the urge for truth comes from; for as yet we have heard only of the obligation imposed by society that it should exist: to be truthful means using the customary metaphors—in moral terms, the obligation to lie according to fixed convention, to lie herd-like in a style obligatory for all.' From 'On truth and lies in an extra-moral sense', in Kaufmann, W. (tr. and ed.), *The Viking Portable Nietzsche*, New York: The Viking Press, 1954, repro. 1969, pp. 46-47.

2   Scholte, R., cited in Edgerton, R.B., *Sick Societies*, New York: The Free Press, 1992, p. 27.

3 *Reason* magazine, June 1999.

4 *Reason*, June 1999.

5 *Independent on Sunday*, 25 May 1997.

6 Dawkins, R.R., *River Out of Eden: A Darwinian View of Life*, London: Weidenfeld & Nicolson, 1995, p. 31.

7 Barry, B., Culture and Equality, An Egalitarian Critique of Multiculturalism, Cambridge: Polity Press, 2001, pp. 284-85.

8 Dawkins, *River out of Eden*, 1995, p. 32.

9 *Daily Telegraph*, 28 June 2004.

10 Leader, the *Guardian*, 9 March 2002.

11 *Daily Telegraph*, 9 September 2004.

12 *The New York Times*, 9 February 1998.

13 Associated Press, 3 November 2002.

14 *The Times*, 11 May 2001.

15 *The Guardian*, 07 June 2004.

5: Rethinking 'The Others'

1 See Hallpike, C.R., *The Foundations of Primitive Thought*, Oxford: Clarendon Press, 1979; Sandall, R., *The Culture Cult: Designer Tribalism and Other Essays*, Colorado: Westview Press, 2001; Whelan, R., *Wild in Woods: The Myth of the Noble Eco-Savage*, London: IEA, 1999.

2 Fromm, E., *The Anatomy of Human Destructiveness*, (1974) London: Penguin edn, 1977, pp. 232-33.

3 Fromm, *The Anatomy of Human Destructiveness*, 1977, pp. 239 & 240.

4 Edgerton, R.B., *Sick Societies*, New York: The Free Press, 1992, p. 140.

5 See Cartledge, P., 'To Die For?', *History Today*, August 2002.

6 *New York Times*, 7 September 2000.

7 Fromm, *The Anatomy of Human Destructiveness*, 1977, pp. 243-54

8 *The Times*, 28 March 2005; *Tribe*, presented by Bruce Parry, broadcast on BBC Two, 17 January 2005.

9 Cited in Levy, N., *Moral Relativism, A Short Introduction*, Oxford: Oneworld, 2002, p. 110.

10 Berndt, C.H. and Berndt, R.M., *The Barbarians*, Middlesex: Penguin, 1971, pp. 76-77.

11 D'Souza, D., *The End of Racism, Principles for a Multiracial Society*, New York: The Free Press, 1995, pp. 30 & 32.

12 See Levinson, D., *Family Violence in Cross-Cultural Perspectives*, Newbury Park, California: Sage, 1989. The only exception appears to be the placid Wape people of Papua New Guinea.

13 Edgerton, *Sick Societies*, 1992, p. 135.

14 D'Souza, *The End of Racism, Principles for a Multiracial Society*, 1995, p. 73.

15 *Times Literary Supplement*, 15 August 2003.

16 Edgerton, *Sick Societies*, 1992, p. 207.

17 Thomas, H., *The Slave Trade, The History of the Atlantic Slave Trade: 1440-1870*, London: Picador, 1997, p. 673.

18 Thomas, *The Slave Trade, The History of the Atlantic Slave Trade: 1440-1870*, 1997, p. 13.

19 *Sunday Telegraph*, 9 September 2001.

20 Sandall, *The Culture Cult*, 2001, p. 113; Barry, B., *Culture and Equality, An Egalitarian Critique of Multiculturalism*, Cambridge: Polity Press, 2001, pp. 253-54.

21 Whelan, *Wild in Woods*, 1999, pp. 31-34.

22 Bailey, R., *Reason*, July 2001

23 Lyons, J., *Chomsky*, London: HarperCollins, 1991, p. 28.

24 *New Scientist*, 19 January 2001.

6: Three Multicultural Paradoxes

1   Cited in the *Daily Telegraph*, 15 December 2001.

2   Hughes, R., *The Culture of Complaint, The Fraying of America*, Oxford University Press, 1993, p. 115.

7: It's My Culture So I'll Do What I Want To

1   *Sunday Telegraph*, 12 September 2004.

2   *Sunday Telegraph*, 9 May 2004.

3   *Guardian*, 16 June 2004.

4   *Independent*, 18 June 2004.

5   *The Times*, 3 March 2005.

6   *The Times*, 13 January 2001.

7   *Guardian*, 6 November 1997.

8   Barry, B., *Culture and Equality, An Egalitarian Critique of Multiculturalism*, Cambridge: Polity Press, 2001, p. 254.

9   *Guardian*, 20 October 1997.

10 *Reason*, April 2002.

11 *New Scientist*, 28 August 2004.

12 *Sunday Telegraph*, 1 February 2004.

13 *Guardian*, 8 April 2002.

14 www.bnp.org.uk logged 18 January 2005.

15 *New York Times*, 14 January 2000.

16 *Observer*, 21 November 2004.

17 *Daily Mail*, 9 October 2003.

18 *Daily Telegraph*, 23 June 2004.

19 *Daily Mail*, 9 October 2003; 16 October 2003.

20 *The Times*, 4 December 2004.

21 *Daily Express*, 1 October 2003.

22 *Observer*, 21 December 2003.

8: The Price of Multiculturalism

1 www.spiked-online.com/Printable/00000002D35E.htm

2 *New Statesman*, 6 October 2004.

3 spiked-online.com, 18 December 2001.

4 *Independent*, 16 April 2003.

5 *Guardian*, 30 November 2004.

6 *News of the World*, 12 September 2004.

7 Letter from a Nigerian teacher to the *London Evening Standard*, 8 September 2004.

8 *Daily Mail*, 12 April 2004.

9 Selbourne, D., *The Losing Battle with Islam: 1947-2004*, uncorrected copy proof, p. 62; forthcoming, October 2005.

10 Selbourne, *The Losing Battle with Islam*, p. 61.

11 *London Evening Standard*, 10 June 2004.

12 Stotsky, S., *Losing Our Language: How Multicultural Classroom Instruction Is Undermining Our Children's Ability to Read Write, and Reason*, New York: Free Press, 1999, pp. 5, 12-13, 41.

13 Sandall, R., *The Culture Cult: Designer Tribalism and Other Essays*, Colorado: Westview Press, 2001, p. 15.

14 See *Hammersmith and Fulham Council Magazine*, 21 October 2004.

15 *London Evening Standard*, 25 July 2004.

16 *Daily Telegraph*, 20 May 2002.

17 *Daily Telegraph*, 18 October 2004.

9: The Challenge to the Left

1   Cited in *Prospect*, December 2000.

2   *Prospect*, February 2004.

3   *Guardian*, 26 February 2004.

4   *Guardian*, 24 February 2004.

5   *Guardian*, 26 February 2004.

6   *Guardian*, 13 February 2004.

7   *The Times*, 18 June 2004.

8   Bronner, S., *Reclaiming the Enlightenment*, New York: Columbia University Press, 2004.

9   Gitlin, T., *The Twilight of Common Dreams: Why America is Wracked by Culture Wars*, New York: Henry Holt, 1995, p. 84.

10 *Guardian*, 15 December 2004.

11 *Guardian*, 31 August 2004.

12 *The Times Educational Supplement*, 23 April 2004.

13 *Guardian*, 29 December 2001.

14 Cited in the *New Statesman*, 19 July 2004.

15 *Observer*, 12 October 2004.

16 *Sunday Telegraph*, 4 July 2004.

17 Barry, B., *Culture and Equality, An Egalitarian Critique of Multiculturalism*, Cambridge: Polity Press, 2001, pp. 11-12.

18 *Mail on Sunday*, 14 March 2004.

19 *Viz*, issue 134, April 2004.

10: The End of Multiculturalism

1 *Catholic Herald*, 22 January 1999.

2 *Islam Under Siege*, Oxford: Polity Press, 2003, p. 117.

3 *News of the World*, 4 June 2000.

4 See Hobsbawm, E. and Ranger, T. (eds), *The Invention of Tradition*, Cambridge University Press, 1983.

5 'The Making of the Caribbean People', in *Spheres of Existence: Selected Writings*, London: Alison and Busby, 1980, p. 179.

6 Fanon, F., *The Wretched of the Earth*, London: Penguin, 1967, p. 253.

7 *The Times*, 29 April 2004.

8 Alibhai-Brown, Y., *Some of My Best Friends Are...*, , London: Politico's, 2004, p. 134.

9 Armstrong, K., *Islam, A Short History*, London: Phoenix, 2001, p. 137.

10 *The Times*, 27 September 2001.

11 *The Times*, 17 March 2004.

12 *Daily Telegraph*, 4 May 2002.

13 *The Times*, 4 December 2004.

14 *Daily Telegraph*, 11 December 2004.

15 *Daily Telegraph*, 23 May 2000.

16 *The Times*, 3 April 2004.

17 *Guardian*, 28 May 2004.

18 *Daily Mail*, 15 March 2005.

19 *Guardian*, 16 March 2005.

20 *Sunday Times*, 5 September 2004.

21 The UK is maybe akin to the two examples above in comprising many nations, but England, Scotland and Wales are not divided by religion any more and they are united by language and same cultural appetites. Northern Ireland is another matter.